REASONS FOR MY HOPE

REASONS FOR MY HOPE

RESPONDING TO NON-CHRISTIAN FRIENDS

BENNO VAN DEN TOREN

MONARCH
BOOKS
Oxford, UK, & Grand Rapids, Michigan, USA

First published in the UK in 2010 by Monarch Books
(a publishing imprint of Lion Hudson plc)
Wilkinson House, Jordan Hill Road, Oxford OX2 8DR, England
Tel: +44 (0)1865 302750 Fax: +44 (0)1865 302757
Email: monarch@lionhudson.com
www.lionhudson.com

ISBN 978 1 85424 863 3

Distributed by:
UK: Marston Book Services, PO Box 269, Abingdon, Oxon, OX14 4YN
USA: Kregel Publications, PO Box 2607, Grand Rapids, Michigan 49501

British Library Cataloguing Data
A catalogue record for this book is available from the British Library.

Printed and bound in the UK by CPI Cox & Wyman, Reading.

Contents

Acknowledgments

This book was originally written in Dutch, and I would like to thank the Dutch League for Interior Mission (Inwendige ZendingsBond – IZB) and the IFES-The Netherlands for their invitation to write it, and for their critical support in the writing process. It was in the Dutch IFES movement and in evangelism within our local church and on campsites supported by the IZB that the main ideas in this book grew through dialogue with both churched and unchurched friends.

Many thanks to Tony Collins of Lion Hudson, who encouraged me to believe that the specific approach to apologetic witness and dialogue presented here could be an important aid for people involved in outreach in our adoptive country. I would like to thank Eveline Cowley-Eland for providing the English translation, and Jan Greenough who shared her great linguistic sensitivity to earth the text in the Anglophone world.

Preface

Recent decades have witnessed a growing openness to discussing questions of religion and faith. Resistance to religious belief is showing significant cracks, and in some places crumbling; there is a growing number of people who have never been inoculated by negative experiences of church. In spite of a few loud voices to the contrary, the idea that science and technical progress are incompatible with belief in God is waning.

However, openness to religion is not automatically openness to Jesus Christ. The fact that many people have no serious experience of the Christian faith also means that it is entirely foreign to them: they have no image at all of what it might mean. It simply doesn't fit their world. Curiosity can therefore be accompanied by misunderstanding. My aim is to help Christians to explain their faith to their non-Christian friends, family and acquaintances, and answer the questions that often arise.

This book is different from other books on the subject: it focuses on understanding the questions and objections that are most often raised in such conversations. Questions which appear similar can have different backgrounds and require different answers; for instance, a question about God and suffering has very different meaning when asked by people acquainted with deep grief. Consequently, this book doesn't aim to give instant answers.

Some readers may at first be discouraged by this approach: it's difficult enough to know how to reply to the most common questions, and now we're being asked to deal with even more.

You might read this book and think: I'll never be able to come up with clever answers like that! It's important to realize that the main thing is not to have a battery of the right arguments and answers, but rather to develop the right attitude: a genuine interest in everyone we meet. The aim of this book is to help people to build their own lives more solidly on the foundation of our faith, which is Jesus Christ. What we discover for ourselves in the process is what we will be able to share with others.

The dialogues in this book are not prescriptive. I'm not saying: "This is how you should do it", but simply giving examples of how the ideas developed here might work out in practice. Everyone will develop their own style. In these dialogues "C" represents the Christian and "N" the person who considers himself or herself a non-Christian. The dialogues are not entirely realistic: both partners appear to speak for slightly longer than normal. Day-to-day conversation allows for more interruptions, but the aim here is to convey the thrust of the argument.

Most of the chapter titles take the form of critical questions about the Christian faith. These are not simply obstacles to belief: they open up opportunities to share who Jesus is. The tone of the dialogue fragments is therefore generally as positive as possible. There's no reason for Christians to behave as if it's difficult to believe in Jesus: when we take the world seriously, having no belief in Jesus raises just as many issues. The critical questions in the chapter headings lead us to positive reasons why we should entrust ourselves to Jesus Christ.

The first two chapters provide a general introduction to what we should look for when dialoguing about questions and objections raised about the Christian faith. If you like approaching issues from a practical angle, you may well prefer to read one or more of the later chapters addressing specific issues before reading the more general opening chapters.

Each chapter concludes with some questions for personal reflection or for group discussion. At the end of the book you will find a list of suggestions for further reading.

Chapter 1

"Why Do You Believe?"

The role of apologetics

As Christians we're always looking for opportunities to talk about Jesus Christ, but it's not always easy to get such conversations started. We hope that the way we live as Christians will provoke questions in the people we meet.

Fortunately opportunities arise wherever we are – at work, in leisure activities or during specific evangelism outreach. But even if people are truly interested in what we have to share, it's not always easy to take the next step. How can we make it clear that the Gospel has meaning for the people we're talking to? And how do we deal with difficult questions about the Christian faith? Can I truly believe in a good God, when there's so much suffering in the world? Why are there so many different religions? What is truth? Why are there so many different churches? Why have so many terrible atrocities been committed in the name of Jesus? How can you believe when so much contradicts your faith?

As Christians we believe in Jesus Christ, that he is the Son of God, and that it's of vital importance to know him. But how do you communicate that to others? These are the questions that "apologetics" deals with. Apologetics is the technical term for the effort to show why belief in Christ and the Gospel is reasonable – and relevant even to those who have not been brought up in the faith. It also addresses the critical questions asked by both non-Christians and Christians. The first two chapters of this book give a general introduction to apologetic witness and to how to handle critical questions about the faith. In this chapter we think about apologetics as a biblical command for our time, and examine its importance by looking at the limitations of what apologetic argument can achieve. In Chapter 2 we will discuss the right attitude to handling difficult questions, and common points of contact and obstacles in conversations about God.

A biblical command

Justifying our faith is not just a Christian hobby, it's a biblical command. The apostle Peter exhorts us to "Always be prepared to give an answer to everyone who asks you to give the reason for the hope that you have. But do this with gentleness and respect" (1 Peter 3:15). This exhortation is not an isolated remark in the Bible. We also have the example of the prophets, the apostles and Jesus himself, who responded to all kinds of questions, both interested and critical, about faith. (For example, Isaiah 41:21–23; John 5:31–36; Acts 17:22–31; 1 Corinthians 15:1–8.)

Peter's exhortation relates closely to the way that God has created humanity and how he wants to deal with us. In the first and greatest commandment, God asks us to love him with all our heart, all our soul and all our mind (Matthew 22:37; in Deuteronomy 6:5 the "mind" is a part of the "heart"). God wants us to serve him with our whole selves, including our intellect. When we come to faith, our lives receive a new direction: we are no longer turned away from God, but towards him (however inadequately our lives may reflect this). Our minds play a part in that change of direction, or conversion. Paul calls us to change our worldly behaviour and "be transformed by the renewing of your mind" (Romans 12:2). When we encourage people in an evangelistic conversation to change the direction of their lives, we also address their thought processes, because the mind plays a crucial role in the discovery of who God is and who he wants to be for them.

In Peter's direction we can unpack three elements of the biblical command to justify our faith. First, Peter tells us to give an answer to everyone "who *asks* you to give the reason for the hope that you have". This implies that the life of a believer should provoke questions. This is a crucial starting-point for all our conversations. However well we may be able to give reasons for our faith, our arguments will be empty and powerless if our faith doesn't show in our lives. When the Christian life is lived to the full, it is seen to be worthwhile and exciting; people will want to know what makes us different.

However, there is no need to wait until we are approached: we can ask people ourselves about the way they live their lives, and start from there to open a discussion about what gives us hope. Hope is perhaps the most important element here. What arouses interest is not simply that we are living a decent life according to God's commandments, but that our life indicates clearly that we have found hope, support, peace and a goal in our lives.

Secondly, Peter speaks of "the hope *that you have*". This is a message that we have processed and taken ownership of. You can't share the faith if it hasn't first become part of your own life. At the very least you must think and live through some of the questions relating to your faith before you are able to justify it to others. So being prepared to give reasons for your faith is not some abstract intellectual affair. For instance, before we can tackle the question of suffering, we must ask ourselves how we have responded to the grief or pain we have experienced or observed. Before we can tackle the issue of other faiths, we must have considered our own encounters with people who live good, faithful lives in obedience to other gods.

That's why the dialogue with non-Christians is always

two-way: when we encourage others to think, we are also made to think ourselves. We are forced to consider what exactly our hope is, and whether it has a solid foundation. Embarking on apologetic discourse involves risk, because sometimes we have to revise our thinking, letting go of some of our deeply held convictions. But if our faith in Jesus Christ is no illusion, we can trust that it is robust. If we continue to return to the foundation of our faith that is Jesus himself, our trust and our hope will only become stronger.

This brings us to a third element of biblical apologetics. Peter does indeed assume that Christian faith and hope is something personal, but it is definitely not merely a personal matter or a subjective feeling. When Peter speaks about hope, he doesn't mean people who are born with an optimistic character or who have decided at a certain moment to look at life from the sunny side. For Peter, hope is always connected with the resurrection of Jesus Christ (1 Peter 1:3, 21). Personal faith is grounded in the hard facts, in the firm reality of God's working in the midst of history (1 Corinthians 15:1–8). That is why we can give reasons for our hope to others. It is not just an idea or emotion, but a reality which concerns everyone.

C. (= Christian): You're talking about having hope for the future as if it's something purely personal, as if everyone should have their own dreams. I wouldn't be able to live with that. If you hope something, you want to have a good reason for it, right? Christians have hope for the future because we know that we don't have to be afraid of dying. Death is the greatest enemy of humanity, and it's been overcome. Jesus is stronger than death, because he died and rose again.

Marks of Christian witness according to 1 Peter 3:15

1. The hope displayed in the lives of Christians is challenging to non-Christians.

2. The Gospel is a message that Christians have come to own for themselves.

3. It is based on an objective truth, independent of the believer.

Apologetics in our time

This kind of witness has always been a mark of faith: in both the Old and the New Testaments, prophets and apostles enter debate and dialogue and give reasons for their belief in God. However, apologetics became even more important in the period of the Enlightenment in the eighteenth century. From that time on, Christians were continually called upon to justify their beliefs. Their faith was summoned before the court of human reason, which was determined to dispense with anything the modern mind found "unreasonable". Some defenders of the faith gave in to this pressure to make it acceptable and diluted their message accordingly. What resulted was a faith without miracles, without a reliable Bible, without the resurrection. But human reason is not adequate for dealing with God: he is so much greater than our minds that we can't just shrink him to fit our small human measures. Moreover, the Bible brings with it a whole vision of its own of what is sensible and intellectually justifiable. We shouldn't let people who have no concept of God determine what counts as reasonable in spiritual matters.

Over the last few decades, the scales seem to have tipped the other way. Many people no longer expect the Christian faith to be reasonable at all. They say that whether you're a Christian or not, belief is a personal matter, influenced by the individual's experiences, feelings and convictions. You may be able to share these convictions and experiences with others, but you can't give arguments for them.

At first glance this development may seem to be an improvement: religious beliefs are permitted again and you're less likely to be attacked for being a Christian. It does, however, have an important consequence. Whenever religious beliefs come up in conversation, you can't get any further than simply exchanging opinions. "We each have our own opinions, so there's no need to discuss or defend them. Let's leave each other free to believe whatever we want, and everyone will be happy." In this culture, Christians will have to go against convention again, but in the opposite direction from before. People have become aware of the limitations of the human mind, but Christians now have to make clear that this doesn't mean that the mind doesn't count at all when talking about God and faith.

As Christians we believe that God gave us our intellectual capabilities, and he asks us to love and serve him "with all our mind". He has given us a very important place in the universe: he created human beings to take responsibility for their thoughts and their deeds. This is clear from the fact that we are not entirely subject to the laws of nature; we are not entirely governed by natural laws or instinctive urges that determine our behaviour, unlike the rest of creation. God guides us by his commandments and promises, but he does not force us to respond in a specific way. However, he does hold us responsible if we refuse to listen: that becomes clear from the condemnations of the prophets and from the judgment of Jesus on those who refuse to believe. This responsibility is implied in the belief that everyone will some day meet God as their judge. This responsibility for our own actions and decisions makes sense only if we have the capacity for making responsible choices: that is why God has given us a mind and a will.

Later on we will see that the human ability to make responsible choices is limited in several ways. People are often trapped by their own feelings, by what drives them and by pressure from other people, but that is definitely not how God meant it to be. In discussions about faith you can help people to free themselves from these pressures: if you as a Christian assume that everyone is responsible for their own attitude towards God, you will need to help them to determine their attitude to God in a responsible manner. Giving them good reasons for your faith encourages this, for responsible choices are those for which you have good reasons. As Christians we are aware, more than most people, of the limits of the human mind, because we are aware of sin and all those other forces that can influence our thinking. But we believe that people are still responsible for their own actions and beliefs and that the Gospel can set them free to act and believe responsibly and rationally.

That is why evangelism is so very different from advertising or from propaganda. Of course we advertise the great God we have. But normal propaganda attempts to manipulate people. As long as people buy the "right" brand of car, clothes or beer, advertisers are not at all interested whether they make their choice on good grounds. Commercials are designed to persuade people to make choices on completely spurious grounds, by making you feel you belong when you buy the right trainers, or by suggesting that if you buy the right car you'll have the same success with women as the driver in the commercial. Evangelism should never manipulate. The evangelist wants people to choose God on good grounds, because he exists, because he is the goal of our life, and because only he can truly redeem us. Good evangelism enables people to decide freely and responsibly to follow Christ. This sets them free from the manipulative pressures and the paralysing subjectivism and relativism in our late-modern society that so often imprison them.

The importance of apologetic witness in evangelism

1. It is a biblical command (1 Peter 3:15).
2. The prophets and apostles set the model.
3. It shows that the Christian faith is not about personal preference but about a truth for everyone.
4. The message of the Gospel is based on an objective reality, a hope that is given to us.
5. God gave us our minds to serve him.
6. In apologetic dialogue we set people free to choose their beliefs and commitments responsibly and on good grounds.
7. Evangelism differs from advertising and propaganda, because it does not manipulate.

Possibilities and limitations

So God has commanded us to witness to our faith and to give a reasonable account of the hope we have, even if confronted with tough questions. Nevertheless, there are limits to the scope of what such apologetic witness can achieve. It's important to understand these limitations, so that we don't give rise to unrealistic expectations in our audience, and so that we won't be disappointed ourselves.

First, belief is the result not only of knowledge and understanding, but of the *will*. It relates to what or whom we love and what's important to us. You can produce books full of sound arguments, you can have fantastic rhetorical skills, but if people don't want to believe, and don't want to give God a place in their life, you'll get nowhere. Saint Augustine said, "reasoning with a stubborn opponent is pointless." The hearer has to be open to belief – or perhaps be broken open by the power of the Holy Spirit. Because belief is related not only to the mind but also to the will, people coming to faith not only need good reasons, they also need to be converted. You can, however, certainly give good reasons why that conversion, that turning towards God, is necessary. We know that it's hard to convince people of what they don't want to see, however true it is and however much they can harm themselves by their stubbornness. That's why the call to conversion remains an essential part of apologetic witness; the prayer for the Holy Spirit, who opens doors and hearts, remains indispensable. "And pray for us, too, that God may open a door for our message, so that we may proclaim the mystery of Christ" (Colossians 4:3).

Belief also has to do with our *feelings*: our emotional world plays a vital role in what we do or don't find acceptable. That doesn't mean that we should stop giving reasons for our faith, but it does mean that all kinds of experiences and feelings will have to be taken into account. People are hardly ever set in motion by theoretical considerations – it is rather their experiences, their desires, their fears and ideals that move them. So these issues must be included in apologetic conversations, to connect them with God. Only when we critically reflect on our experiences and feelings can we discover which experiences lead us to God and which lead us astray; which desires are right, which fears are justified and which are not.

C.: You say you can't accept that we need God to save us – but you seem to feel that very strongly. How come you're so absolute?... Of course your feelings are important, but you should look at them with a critical eye. In my own life I know my feelings have led me the wrong way time and again. I've thought I didn't need any help, but looking back, I've seen that I did. Can you relate to that?

Next, there's the issue of *the limitation of our understanding*. When we attempt to give reasons for our faith, we need to realize that we can never fully understand God, because he is infinitely greater than we are (Deuteronomy 29:29; Isaiah 55:8–9; 1 Timothy 6:16). Everything we know about God is blurred by our weakness and sin (1 Corinthians 13:12). God has made his purposes known to us, but much of what happens in our lives will remain unclear.

Finally, there's the issue of the *nature of our knowledge of God*. We must realize that we know God in a special way, the way that's appropriate for this very special relationship. There's nothing wrong with that: the way I "know" my wife is different from the way I "know" a mathematical proposition. It's important to understand this, because often people ask for the kind of knowledge about God that isn't possible. "I'm willing to believe in God, if you can prove to me that he exists." Often they ask for some sort of scientific evidence, the type of proof that works in our visible world – but in fact, in only very limited aspects of our visible world. In a courtroom, for example, you need a completely different kind of evidence: reliable witnesses.

I don't doubt at all that my wife loves me, but it's impossible to prove that in a scientific way. And I don't need to. I know it, because she tells me herself and because I trust her. A "proof of love" is a different kind of proof from the evidence that stones always fall downwards, or the kind of proof that is demanded in a court of law. That's also how it works with faith. We need to look for the type of evidence that's appropriate for knowing God. "Faith comes from hearing" (Romans 10:17), but it is not less certain for relying on "hearing", for it goes back to reliable witnesses, to a convincing declaration of love. Therefore "faith is being sure of what we hope for and certain of what we do not see" (Hebrews 11:1). We will elaborate on this issue of the evidence for the Christian faith in Chapter 6.

These four limitations of what apologetic witness can achieve don't mean that the command to give reasons for your faith should not be taken seriously. They do mean, however, that a balanced and rounded apologetic witness should address the people whom we meet as whole, entire and integrated persons. We must be aware of the friends we engage in dialogue as people who are responsible for their own convictions; as people with free will; with all sorts of feelings and experiences; as human beings who have been created to know God, yet who will never fully understand him.

Questions for group discussions or personal reflection

1. Are you ever confronted with difficult questions about the Christian faith? How do you feel when that happens? (Are you happy to find an opportunity for conversation? Slightly scared? Does it make you aware of similar questions of your own?) How do you react?

2. What do you feel you need to know in order to answer such questions? You could write down your ideas, and see how far this book helps you.

3. Why does God ask us to serve him with our mind (Matthew 22:37), and tell us that our minds should be renewed (Romans 12:2)? What does that mean for us?

4. Peter's exhortation to "always be prepared to give an answer to everyone who asks you to give the reason for the hope that

you have" suggests three things: (a) hope must be visible in our lives; (b) hope must be something that we have made our own; and (c) hope is not just about subjective feelings, but links us to a reality outside ourselves. Which of these three elements is most difficult for you? Do you see potential for growth in that area?

5. What do you consider the biggest obstacles for apologetic witness nowadays? How can we overcome them?

6. What is the difference between evangelism and advertising? How can we make that clear?

Chapter 2

"Can't You Understand?"

Developing the right attitude

Coping with difficult questions in evangelism is not simply a matter of knowing the right answers: it's more important to have the right attitude. Preparing a set of good responses is insufficient, because new questions will come up all the time – questions to which you may not know the answer, and perhaps never will. And different people can ask what seems like a similar question – but with a very different emotional or intellectual charge. The same answer may not be appropriate in every situation.

Your own life of faith

Having the right attitude begins with the way you deal with your own faith, the place in your own life which you make for your relationship with God. This is not just true for apologetic witness, but for all sharing of our faith. Before you can justify your faith to others, you need to ask yourself *what* you believe and *why* you believe it – giving an account of "the hope that you have". That seems to be a lot to ask of us. We probably have many questions about our own faith, and there is so much we don't understand ourselves. But our job is not to know everything or be able to explain all, but to be able to share the little we know about God and Jesus, to say why it's so important for us and why it gives us so much to hold on to. Our limitations can actually be a help to other people, if we make it clear that we don't have to know and understand everything before we can believe. We can show how we deal with the problems of faith.

But even though God can make good use of the little we know, we shouldn't be content to stay where we are. If we want other people to take these issues seriously, we must take them seriously too. What do we really mean when we speak about God? Why do we believe it's good to go to church? If we confront these questions squarely, our conversations will enrich us too, and help us grow in our life with God.

When we talk about what we believe, we are not just citing our own opinions, but expressing the faith taught in the Bible. Nevertheless, our friends hear it from our lips, in our own words. That has the huge advantage that they aren't just hearing an ancient story, but sharing in the real experience of someone's present life: they perceive immediately how much Jesus Christ means to us. However, that means we'll have to learn how to put into words our love for God and for Jesus. What do we actually believe about Jesus? And why is he so important to us?

We are used to talking about these things within the church, in the Bible study group, the evangelism committee and lots of other places. We talk about "sin" and "atonement", about "God's care" and about "new life". Yet outside the church such words are almost meaningless, so we need to think carefully about what we mean. It's good practice, even among believers, to try to use less "churchy" language. In the secular world it sounds like so much hocus-pocus, and it doesn't make much difference whether you use the insider language of the King James Version or of the New Wine Network. Most people have no concept of these religious terms, so what are they going to make of them? Sometimes it may help to go back to the basic images that form the roots of some of the central biblical terms. Different words for "sin" in the Bible refer, for example, to "transgression" of the law of God, to the "godlessness" of a life without God, to the "filth" of a life corrupted by sin, or to our "missing the goal" when we miss out on God's great project for our lives.

If you try to translate your faith like this, you'll discover certain things. You realize how precious these important words are to us, how specialized their meaning, and how difficult it is for us to manage without them. It helps you to see what a huge step it is for people to comprehend the Christian faith when they don't understand the language we use. Perhaps you'll also notice that you often use words whose meaning you can't easily explain. When you try to translate it into everyday language, you'll start to see more clearly what your faith means.

We need to look for words not only to say *what* we believe, but also to say *why* we believe. This is especially important nowadays, when so many people feel you can believe whatever you want, or whatever faith you've been raised in, but that you don't need to have reasons for those beliefs. Of course it is true that many Christians grew up in the faith, and learned it from their parents. However, at some point they needed to take responsibility for their own choice to follow Jesus, and to trust God. When you start to put your reasons for that into words, it becomes your personal story, because that road to personal commitment has been different for everyone. Maybe you experienced God's guidance in your life. Maybe you discovered that the Bible really had something to say about the world. Maybe you realized that Jesus was different from all the other ways that promise salvation. Or maybe you were impressed with the lives of Christians you met or read about.

The question of why you believe will always get a personal answer, coloured by your own life. We all discover Jesus in our own way, and learn how important he is and how to entrust our lives to him. At the same time it's good to look for answers that you can share with others when those conversations with non-believers arise. In the end we believe in Jesus because we have come to see that what's been said about him is *true*, that he is the Son of God, and because his existence is of *vital importance* for everyone. That will have to come out of our personal story. In several of the following chapters reasons will be given why we as Christians believe in Jesus as the Son of God. It is good to take time to discover what those reasons mean to you personally.

> ***C.:*** *The stories of Christ's resurrection played an important role for me personally. When I started to ask myself if everything my parents and the church told me about God was actually true, I started looking at the reports of the resurrection in the Bible. I was thoroughly impressed with how trustworthy they appeared to be, even after serious critical study. And if Jesus really did rise from the dead, if we have good reason to believe that, then the implications are huge. He really does have all power in heaven and on earth, because he's stronger than death. It really is safe to entrust myself to him.*

Listening

A conversation is an exchange between at least two people, each with their own life, their own thoughts, convictions, ideals and worries. In an evangelistic conversation the thoughts and experiences of the other person are at least as important as your own. In fact, the other person's life is much more important, because you're trying to make a connection between them and the Gospel. You are only important in so far as you, with your experiences, are a bridge between that person and the Lord Jesus. The other person is central to the conversation, because the crucial question is what God has to do with their life, and whether it's possible for them to believe in God. That's why you'll have to search for the uniquely personal questions they have, for the obstacles to believing they may encounter, and for the clues to the Gospel that become visible in their life.

Jesus himself could summarize his message in one sentence: "Repent, for the kingdom of heaven is near!" (Matthew 4:17). But for every person that he met, he had something else to say, something that spoke exactly the right words into their life. In the same way, we should get to know the people we're speaking to, so we know who they are and where they are in life. We can only do that successfully if we really listen to them, and that means listening not only to what they say, but to what they *don't say*, hearing what lies behind their questions and criticisms: anger, grief, openness, resistance or indifference.

Sometimes the same question can mean very different things. Often people mention the things churches and Christians get wrong. How they talk about this matters a great deal. Perhaps they've personally had a bad experience of the church. On the other hand, it may be a much more theoretical question: how can I believe in a God who changes people if many Christians lead such disappointing lives? Or maybe it's just an attempt to avoid a more serious conversation, because most people know this is a hard question to answer. Clearly, you need to react differently in these different situations. But you won't know what's really going on if you don't enquire further, and really listen to what's been said.

C.: You're saying that so fiercely, that Christians are as bad as other people. Have you had experiences with Christians that make you think that?

Careful listening is not easy; too often we're already thinking about what we're going to say next, rather than listening to what's being said. Listening is a skill you have to learn, but it's one you can learn. Try to practise the following strategies to improve your listening skills:

- Let the other person finish what they're saying, and pause before you react. The difference between a heated debate and a real conversation is mainly how much space you give the other person.
- Consciously avoid thinking about your response while the other person is still talking; wait and ask yourself first what they really mean.
- Ask yourself the question: why do they say that? What lies behind the words – which feelings, experiences, basic assumptions and motives? Make sure you're listening out of true interest.
- Ask clarifying questions to find out exactly what they mean.
- Be reflective by repeating the thoughts of the other person in your own words: "Am I right in thinking that you...?"
- Never use listening as a strategic weapon that will help you find the weak points in someone else's defence, but as an expression of true interest in and true respect for the other person.

When people notice that you're genuinely interested in them, and not only in yourself and your own ideas, they'll be much more open to what you have to say.

Arguments and motives

It's important to listen carefully in order to discover what really motivates other people. Most people won't say directly what motivates their rejection of the Christian faith. The strange thing is that people often list arguments that are not at all important to them. Suppose someone at church asks me to do something I really don't feel like doing. Of course I can give reasons why I can't do it: "I'm not available on Wednesday evenings." But if that problem's solved, I give another reason why I'm not the right person for the job: "I don't have enough experience." Or possibly: "I don't have transport." We keep on changing arguments if they turn out to be unsound, as long as our real motives don't come into the open. Maybe I just don't want to work with the other person who's already involved. It's more often than not the deeper motive that's decisive, rather than more superficial reasons. "Motives" are precisely that: the feelings that "move" us to take a certain position, while "reasons" are the arguments we marshal to defend the position we have already taken.

That's how it is with many people who reject the Christian faith. The arguments they use are sometimes just means to protect themselves. As long as their motives remain intact, nothing will change. If their arguments appear unsound they will just exchange them for others. It can cost you lots of time to refute criticisms that are actually not at all relevant to the person you're talking to. It's only when you find out what the real problems and objections are that the conversation can become meaningful, not a fake exchange of ideas that don't touch on the real issues. That's what often happens with what I call a "dog's bone question" – like a dog, you've been tempted with a bone, and the questioner is hoping you'll be busy gnawing away at these side-issues and not approach their real problems. It's only when you begin to lay bare deeper motives that you can enter into a true dialogue. You can begin to query whether those motives – such as "I can't accept someone else telling me what's good for me" – are at all healthy. It's also possible that these motives unexpectedly turn out to be valuable and justified in the light of the Gospel: "Of course you should be angry about the suffering in the world!"

Attitude in relation to content

Our own attitudes are also important, because in our manner we can show something of the content of the Gospel. Conversely, our words can be completely stripped of their power if we assume an attitude that is contrary to their content.

Our attentive listening and our reactions can demonstrate that the Gospel is not just a message about general truths, but about something of vital importance to us personally. On the other hand, it's difficult to persuade other people that God is interested in them and accepts them if we show that we aren't really interested in their life, but only in the story we want to tell.

If we wish to ask others to face Jesus' claims honestly and to overcome all kinds of resistance in their life, we have to demonstrate honesty in our conversation. This means that we'll sometimes have to admit that we don't know all the answers. That's not a bad thing. Our relationship with God is a personal one, a relationship of trust – we trust him enough to go forward without understanding everything.

On occasions, we may even have to be sharp and critical, just as Jesus could be sharp if people hid behind their questions in order to avoid facing the reality of God in their own life.

C.: I don't know that it's helpful to keep going back to that church warden who disappointed you so badly when you were young. It was wrong, but you can't let your whole life be influenced by an experience from so long ago. Wouldn't it be better to ask the question whether you could start all over again with God?

Obstacles as points of contact

Listening carefully is vital. It's only when we listen and ask what people mean, and discover the emotional charge behind their ideas, that we can see where the obstacles lie, and where there are points of contact for the Gospel. For instance, many people have a longing for peace, safety and security, or a longing for happiness which they feel no one can fulfil: those are points of contact from which you can explain the relevance and truth of the Gospel. Many people outside the church have great admiration for the person of Jesus; others have feelings of awe at the miracle of creation, or of insecurity, or of the fragility of life.

You have to listen carefully to identify these obstacles to belief, because they may be buried at a very deep level. What is amazing is that many of these issues are not just problems to be overcome, but they can be points of contact and great starters for a constructive conversation. Let us consider different types of obstacles with that possibility in mind.

A great number of critical questions are provoked because people have *wrong ideas* about the Christian faith. These offer good opportunities to explain what the Gospel is really about.

*N. (= **non-Christian**): I think the church is a rather good institution. It helps people to care for each other. But I don't need the church for that. I can help people without going to church.*

C.: I'm glad you feel church is a caring place. But church is about much more than making us better people: it's about God setting us free of the things that keep us captive – guilt, fear, wrong choices. It's not just about the way we relate to other people, but about how we relate to God. Does God mean anything to you?

Some questions arise from the fact that people ask you *why* you believe. How do you know God exists? Why do you believe that the Bible is the Word of God? How can you be convinced that Jesus Christ is the only way to God? Do you have good reasons for that? Sometimes these questions are very critical, because they assume that you won't have good reasons. Sometimes people are genuinely bemused about how you can believe such things. These questions provide especially good opportunities to make it clear that our faith has a firm foundation. "We did not follow cleverly invented stories" (2 Peter 1:16).

Among the more theoretical questions there are also those which arise from all sorts of things that people know or think they know, and which they can't combine with the Christian faith. These may, for example, refer to the divisions between churches, to the scarcely convincing lives of Christians, to the suffering in the world, to science, to other religions, to the character of the Bible. These are issues that we can find quite difficult ourselves at times, and to which we will have to find answers. But often those answers help us move beyond apologizing for our weaknesses, and show instead how all these questions can give us openings to point to the greatness and depth of the Gospel message. In the next chapters we will look for answers to these and similar questions.

Many obstacles have to do with specific *experiences* that people have had in their lives. In that case people are not just asking a theoretical question: they have strong feelings. Perhaps they are angry or disappointed, afraid or ashamed about something. We've already mentioned the suffering people may have experienced in their lives, or disappointing experiences they may have had in the church. Such obstacles can become the starting-point for a really positive conversation, when we try to make a connection between those events and who God is: a God who specifically wants to be involved with human suffering, and a God who thankfully is very different from his ground-crew.

Sometimes the feelings that keep people from believing are such deeply ingrained *emotional scars* that they can't just set them aside, even if they want to. You sometimes hear: "I wish I could believe, but I just can't." That's when a process of healing is needed. This can sometimes take a long time, and it goes beyond the purpose of this publication. It is mentioned here only so you can take into account that this may play a role in the background of apologetic conversations. In Wim Rietkerk's book, *If Only I Could Believe!*, you can find out more about addressing such emotional scars.

Obstacles can also derive from *unwillingness* to believe. Some people continue to criticize the Christian faith and don't hear what you say, because they don't want to listen. But why don't they want to? Sometimes it can clear the air to just put the question on the table: "Would you like to believe, or not at all? Why not?" Or: "If I could answer all the questions that you're asking, would you want to become a Christian?" In this way you can approach these obstacles rooted in the will, and maybe erode some of the resistance in that area. In the end a measure of unwillingness remains in every human being and we have to ask people to convert from that unwillingness – just as we do ourselves, again and again: "If anyone chooses to do God's will, he will find out whether my teaching comes from God or whether I speak on my own" (John 7:17).

We can see how critical questions themselves offer plenty of possibilities to engage in conversation in a positive way. For that matter, it's important not to sidetrack too much, but to look for ways to return to the central issues of the Gospel. Who is God? How does he deal with us? Who is Jesus and what is His relationship with us? We shouldn't do this with the secret intention of sweeping difficult questions under the carpet, but so that the light of the Gospel itself may fall on them. When we face questions like this in a positive way, there are important consequences for the conversation: a positive attitude prevents us from being too defensive, too protective or from apologizing all the time. If we are honest, we do need to apologize for our fallible church, but we don't need to defend God or apologize for him. There is every reason to trust him and we can justify that in full confidence.

Not against, but alongside each other

One of the most important obstacles to an open and fruitful conversation is our human reluctance to admit that we're wrong. In religious discussions it's easy to end up opposing each other. I have been guilty of that, trying to persuade other people that they're wrong. Of course the result is that people only search harder for reasons to defend their position. People really listen only when they don't feel threatened; when they feel they can be enriched if they consider carefully what's being shared. That's why you need to try to come alongside your conversation partner. Compare the following two responses to a question about the resurrection, and ask yourself how you would react if you weren't a Christian.

> *N.: You keep talking about the resurrection of Jesus, but I can't really believe a dead person can come to life again. That just doesn't happen, does it?*

> *C. (1): People often say that, but it's silly. Just because something doesn't normally happen, that doesn't mean it's impossible!*

C. (2): I can understand you thinking it's impossible to return from the dead. The people who first heard about it, and even the ones who saw Jesus after his resurrection, were equally shocked and couldn't believe it. There's every reason not to just accept it. Still, there are plenty of other things that you can't imagine at first, but that turn out to be true after all. We could look at the Bible reports of the resurrection together, and see if they seem trustworthy.

It is important not only to try coming alongside the other person, but also to show that what you have to say in the end is in line with what they are looking for. Of course, it's true that in profound ways the Gospel message goes against what we, as sinful human beings, want. We don't want to live by God's grace and obey him. But in a conversation you don't have to emphasize that – conversion is hard enough as it is! But on another level the Gospel provides an answer to the deepest questions of our life. It's not called *Evangel*, "Good News", for no reason.

Anyway, it's normally almost impossible to let go of a certain conviction if you don't feel that there's any alternative. While you haven't seen anything better, you hold on to what you have and defend your position. That's why criticizing people's ideas doesn't persuade them: they won't change their minds until they've understood that the Christian faith offers an attractive and realistic alternative. Therefore it's much better to begin by inviting them to get to know the Christian faith, to discover how Christians view the world, and show the sense, reality and power of the Gospel, without criticizing their convictions. They will be more prepared to listen to criticism when they've more idea about the alternative. For many people, conversion to the Christian faith is a gradual process; for a while they'll be living more or less in two worlds, viewing reality with old and with new eyes. They may have been socializing with Christians for a while, gone to church every now and then, even gone to a Bible study group or exploratory course, before the moment arrives when the new view appears so convincing that they can release the old one.

Part of this resistance to open conversations about the Gospel can be the fact that even when people begin to recognize the truth of the Christian faith, they don't want to admit that this is something important they've been ignoring, while others were ahead of them. When conversations come to this point, it's sometimes possible to help people by referring to your own experiences, times when you have made mistakes and been helped by others to find the right way again. By describing the great moment when everything was straightened out and you were able to contemplate the possibility of making things right with God, you may make it easier for them to take the painful step of recognizing their own shortcomings.

Seven types of obstacles ... and how you can deal with them

1 Mistaken ideas about God and the Christian faith.

1 Explain what the Gospel says.

2 Demanding to know "why".

2 Explain the foundation of our faith.

3 Ideas that conflict with faith.

3 You may need to refute these, clarify them or show how they have their place within the Christian faith.

4 Experiences that conflict with faith.

4 Try to connect these experiences with God.

5 Emotional barriers to trusting God.

5 Speak about and search for healing.

6 Unwillingness.

6 Point out the necessity of conversion.

7 Finding it difficult to admit you're wrong.

7 Get alongside your conversation partner and share your own experience.

Questions for group discussions and personal reflection

1. What were the most important reasons why you started believing in Christ? Do you think that non-Christians can relate to them?

2. Is it possible to probe in a sensitive and respectful way for the deeper and more hidden motivations and convictions behind people's questions? Can you think of ways to do this?

3. Jesus was often asked trick questions by people whose motives were not genuine interest. Can you name examples? Can you think of conversations you've had (about belief or anything else) where with hindsight you feel that someone's true motives didn't surface? How can you handle these?

4. Many people aren't even aware of the main hindrances that hold them back from accepting Christ. How can we help them to discover these?

5. What do you think is more common: inability to believe or unwillingness to believe? How can we recognize both? How would you deal with someone whose personal history prevented them from believing? What could you say to someone who is unwilling to believe?

6. Compare the two answers to the remark about the resurrection. Try to think of a few other examples of critical questions about God, and how your answers can place you either alongside or in opposition. Try to formulate your response so that it is inviting rather than criticizing.

A listening exercise

Listening is something you must learn. If you're working through this book in a group, you could actually practise listening to each other, perhaps by discussing Question 1 in pairs. Take it in turns to answer, with the second person saying nothing until the first has finished talking, and genuinely believes he or she has been listened to and understood. Check this by reporting back to the group what your partner has said.

If you are reading this book alone, you could resolve to spend some time every day this week in really listening to at least one person you meet. This seems like a really trivial task, but you'll find it isn't always easy.

A reflection exercise

When we speak about obstacles to believing and points of contact with the faith, the danger of projection is huge. We may have discovered in our own life a certain resistance to God, and as we have worked through that, God has touched us in a certain way. The danger is that we then assume that other people's obstacles will be comparable to our own. We project our own difficulties and history onto them. Try to describe to yourself the issues in your own life that kept you back from giving yourself to God and the way that God has dealt with them. Try also to express the way in which, in your personal life story, the Gospel connected to some of your deep longings, convictions or fears. When we are aware of ourselves we will be better able to help others with their problems. At the same time we'll be much better able to realize that not everyone is the same as us, and that God approaches each of us in specific ways.

Chapter 3

"What About Suffering?"

The problem of pain

N.: She was my brother's little daughter. She was only three years old when she got leukaemia. My brother was a Christian and they prayed a lot for her. When things went better they thanked God. But six months later she died anyway. I can't believe in God if he allows that. She hadn't done anything wrong. And it's such a lovely family. They're the last people to deserve this.

The question of suffering is the most common and one of the most difficult questions you'll encounter in conversations about the Gospel. For believers it's not a strange question. The Psalms, part of the life of the Jewish people and of the church for many centuries, show that through the ages this question has been a challenge to faith for believers. Where there is a crisis of faith, however, there is also a longing to find God, and to hold on to him despite everything. The question of suffering is also raised by people who have given up on God, and who find it one of the best arguments to defend their position. That's why this problem is sometimes called "the bastion of atheism".

The fact that this issue can be raised by so many people, in such widely differing ways, is an indication that here is an area where it's especially important to question closely and to listen attentively to what is meant.

The experiences behind the question

Obviously people encounter suffering in many different ways, so the question can take on different nuances, and so the answers we give will need to change accordingly. Only you can decide what kind of answer will serve best in any situation.

First, we need to be aware that a question couched in even the most general terms can hide very personal experiences. When you're discussing faith with people you don't know well, they usually outline their objections in very general terms. The only way to find out what's really going on is to probe further. Giving too swift a response will only provoke a defensive attitude: "Christians really don't understand what it's all about." However, if people discover that you're truly interested in them, even in their difficult experiences, they'll be prepared to have a deeper and more personal conversation.

> **C.:** *You're very definite when you say there can't be a God if he allows suffering. You sound almost angry. I get the feeling this really affects you. Have you seen much suffering in your own life?*

Whenever people have been deeply affected by suffering, their experiences still differ. If they are willing to share their story we must try to empathize with what makes it so painful to them now. Is their concern for other people – the suffering of the innocent? Was their own suffering unbearable? Are they disappointed in God because they prayed to no avail? Or are they distressed by the suffering in the world at large, even if their own life is reasonably comfortable? What is it that affects them most – the injustice of suffering or the hopelessness of living in a world that doesn't seem to have a future? When we really take the time to listen, to ask further questions and to empathize, our attitude will already be reflecting something of the character of God, so later on we can more convincingly say that he truly cares about our pain, even if there is a great deal we don't understand about it.

When this issue arises, it doesn't always come out of a personal confrontation with suffering, or out of a painful awareness of the suffering in the world. Sometimes the question is purely an intellectual one. "How can Christians believe there's a God who is both loving and almighty? Such a God would have the power to end all the suffering in the world. Therefore God doesn't exist." This kind of question can genuinely worry people and be a serious hindrance to belief. We mustn't be tempted to think that it's only when it arises from personal experience that the question is a serious one.

Whatever the origin of the question, it's important to listen carefully to it, to see in which *direction* the person who asks the question is moving. Is this someone who is seeking God, and open to an encounter with him? Or is it someone moving away from God, who has written him off and who is being pushed further away when she considers the question of suffering? Clearly, in the first case the person will be more willing to search for an answer. Sometimes it can be good just to ask that question.

C.: I hope you won't find this too personal a question, but if there were a clear answer to this issue, what would you like it to be? Would life be more bearable for you if there were a God? Or would you actually be rather annoyed if God seemed to exist after all?

N.: Well, I've never really thought about it like that. I suppose I wouldn't like to think there was someone who wanted to interfere with my life and impose all sorts of rules on me. I'm doing pretty well by myself. I like it better like this.

Sometimes suffering is raised as a "dog's bone" question – the sort your friend hopes will keep you busy for a while. Non-

Christians generally know quite well that suffering is a problem for Christians. If the conversation about faith has taken a turning that's uncomfortable for them, or if they really don't like talking about God and Jesus in a personal way, then they look for a way to divert it onto a safer track. Occasionally it's good to respect this, but sometimes it can also be good to probe a bit further. I remember a conversation in which I felt we came closest to the heart of the matter when we began talking about how God was interested in my friend and wanted a relationship with him. That was the point at which he suddenly raised the question of suffering, I believe as a diversion.

> *N.: You say God is interested in us, but how can He be, when there's so much suffering in the world?*

> *C.: That's a huge question, and Christians have always wrestled with it. We can talk a bit more about that. But first I'd like to finish what we were talking about: would it make a difference to your life if God was interested in you personally?*

What do you think about the following reaction?

> *C.: You've brought up the issue of suffering. I hope you don't mind if I'm a bit direct, but is that really a question for you, or do you know the answer already?*

> *N.: Of course it's not a question. There just is no God.*

> *C.: That's not as clear for everyone. What makes you so certain of that?*

What's the background to this question about suffering?

1. The person I'm speaking with has been personally affected by suffering in his own life or he is pained by the suffering in the world.

2. Suffering is an intellectual problem: how can you believe that an almighty and good God exists when there's so much suffering?

3. It's a "dog's bone" question to avoid a real conversation.

Different biblical responses to suffering

The question of suffering doesn't have to lead people away from God. The vehemence, depth and seriousness with which the question "Why?" is asked in the Bible itself show that we can bring it before God. Think of Job, of the Psalms, of Paul's thorn in the flesh, of Jesus' own "Why?" on the cross. For many people, the question "Why?" can be a good way into the world of the Bible.

Just as the question of suffering may have different origins, so we don't find just one sort of "Why?" and one sort of answer in the Bible. The Bible has something to say to very different people in diverging situations. Therefore, the challenge for us is not to find an answer that's absolutely conclusive and fully satisfying. If the person we're talking to demands that we deliver such an answer, we can only ask them how they cope now: have they already found an answer that satisfies them completely? The Bible doesn't provide a conclusive answer, but it does provide guidance that helps me to cope with life from day to day. And because the Bible speaks to so many situations, we have faith that there is no suffering so deep that God's message cannot reach us in it.

We can discern in the Bible five different kinds of answer to help us walk alongside people on the road where God is leading them.

Human responsibility

The first biblical answer lies in the personal responsibility of humankind. The first mention of evil in the Bible is not one where man calls God to account ("Why do you allow this?") but where God calls humankind to account ("Adam, where are you?", cf. Genesis 3:9). That is part of the uniqueness of the biblical understanding of evil. Evil is not necessary. It could just as well not have existed. It exists because human beings wanted to shape their life without God, because they did not want to live dependent on God and trusting him. Because humans are designed to live in an obedient and loving relationship with God, they bring evil into the world when they refuse this relationship. This evil isn't just an arbitrary punishment from God. Humans simply cannot live properly without God and cannot find fulfilment outside this relationship: that's not how we are made, and that's not how we are meant to live.

Apparently God wanted to take the risk of creating humanity with the ability to respond to his love in freedom, but therefore also with the ability to reject it. God is looking for a relationship of love with us. That's why we can find very good and appealing examples in the realm of human relationships which show that love, freely given, is worth the risk of rejection.

C.: Why is it so important to me that my wife has chosen to share her life with me? Because she did it of her own free will – she could have chosen someone else! As a father, it's more important for me to develop a good bond with my son, than with my car. I care more if my son does something to please me, than if my car does what I expect it to do. Because however difficult it may be, you have to give your children space to choose their own life. And if the children want to allow the parents into their lives, it is their choice.

Of course, since humans were created, the freedom they have to organize their own lives has become compromised. Lots of evil in our lives doesn't happen because of our own wrong choices but because of others. And even when we do evil ourselves, sometimes we feel as if we're compelled by forces that seem stronger than us: when we harm someone with our angry words, our anger may have strong and hidden roots that can be found. We know how some people go from bad to worse and ruin their own lives and those of others – but we know it can be because of their upbringing, because of the company they keep, or because of certain problems in their life. For that matter the Bible is very realistic when it sees humans not simply as responsible for evil, but also as victims of evil, even of the evil in themselves: we have become imprisoned by sin. This is precisely why we need Jesus not only to reconcile us with God, but also to set us free by overcoming evil (see Matthew 12:28–29; Romans 6:6). However, all this does not diminish the fact that the responsibility for evil does not lie primarily with God, but with humanity itself; it is out of love that God gave us free will and continues to hold us responsible for how we relate to him and the people around us.

This reference to freedom and love is very appealing for modern people, and provides an answer to the more intellectually formulated question of suffering – the reproach that the existence of an almighty and loving God and the reality of evil can't be combined. God can allow the possibility of evil, because otherwise free will wouldn't be possible. The most basic response to this intellectual problem is that the worst suffering is caused by people. Even many seemingly natural disasters like the floods in Bangladesh and the desertification of the Sahel can be largely traced back to bad management of the good creation God gave us. Sometimes, however, we need to continue the dialogue to cover the natural evils for which man does not have direct responsibility: earthquakes, disease, and the cruelty of the animal world. Here we could point to the fact that according to Genesis 3, God has linked the fate of the rest of creation to humanity, which makes us responsible for the curse that lies over the creation. Yet even so, this is not a complete answer.

It's important to refer to the freedom and responsibility of humankind, because the discussion about the "Why?" of suffering can often move towards reproaching God for the state of the world, leaving humans out of the picture completely. When we talk about suffering in biblical terms the focus is not primarily on a God who lets people suffer, but rather on people who grieve and hurt God, because they've made such a terrible mess of God's good creation.

C.: Yes, sometimes I feel I want to reproach God about that. But whenever I look critically at myself, I realize God has many more reasons to reproach me. When I hurt the people around me by my behaviour, I hurt God, because he wants the best for them. And I hurt God when I try to live my life without him, because he longs to have a personal relationship with me. And we owe him that relationship, because he created us.

Approached like this, the issue of suffering need not make us defensive. Instead, it offers an opportunity to point to God's love for us, and to mention our need for forgiveness.

Suffering for a purpose

The idea of human responsibility for the suffering in the world can be helpful for some people. However, this rather general view can be wide of the mark when people's real concern is their own suffering, or if they've been intensely affected by the suffering of someone close to them. Their problem is not so much that pain exists, but that *I* have suffered pain. Why does it hit me? Why her? Do we deserve it more than others? In these cases it's important to discover why the pain is felt so deeply, and which other biblical answers can open a way to the heart of this very personal question.

A second way in which the Bible speaks about suffering is as something God can use to create something good, often to teach us more of what life is about. One of the reasons why modern people find suffering so unbearable is that personal happiness has become the highest goal of life. Happiness is described in very precise terms, in enjoying relationships, family life, meaningful work and so on. Although these are things Christians consider to be valuable, their value is limited. We can probe a little further to discover what people consider to be the true meaning of life.

C.: Am I right in saying that the most important thing for you is to have good personal relationships, with a great partner?... And you find it unbearable that it's exactly in that area that things in your life have gone wrong? It's terrible, I know, and you've been badly hurt. But imagine for a bit that God has something much more beautiful in store for you, a life that surpasses your greatest expectations. If everything in our life went the way we want it to, we might never get to something even better – a relationship with God. In my own life...

When we speak about God using the difficult things in our lives, however, we must be very careful. It's too easy to give people the impression that God wants there to be evil in our lives. It's possible that God has sometimes deliberately led things this way, but I believe that most of the time he is using things that actually hurt him because they're wrong – things like diseases, broken relationships, grief or unemployment. "In all things God works for the good of those who love him" (Romans 8:28). Evil things go against God's good intentions for his world, but in relationship with him they can work for good; they can motivate us to search more single-heartedly for the best there is – our relationship with him. Many people will admit that their problems have taught them something important – for example, that good relationships are more important than material possessions. That is a discovery that comes from God. But God goes further than that; he wants to teach us that a good relationship with him makes life much more meaningful, even though we find it so easy to leave him out of our lives.

Eternal joy

God has the power to transform even the difficult things in our lives for good. This becomes even clearer when we look at the third answer the Bible gives to the question of why there is suffering. Romans 8 says: "I consider that our present sufferings are not worth comparing with the glory that will be revealed in us" (verse 18). As Christians we measure our suffering in this life against the joy of the future we expect to spend with God, when he creates a new heaven and a new earth. That points up even more sharply how valuable suffering can be, if it opens our hearts to something even more precious: a relationship with Jesus. Even a glimpse of that future shows us suffering in a different light. It's put into perspective, because it's seen against a greater reality.

Gavin Reid, the former bishop of Maidstone, once interviewed a boy in a church service. The boy had fallen downstairs as a baby, and had spent most of his life in hospital. Still, the boy said, he believed that God was fair. The bishop interrupted him and asked: "How old are you?"

"Seventeen," said the boy.

"How long have you spent in hospital?"

"Thirteen years," came the answer.

"And do you think that fair?" asked the bishop.

The boy answered: "God has all eternity to make it up to me."[1]

God's healing hand

In any case, we're not just waiting for that future. There is a fourth biblical response: prayer. We can pray now for the wounds that life has inflicted to be healed; for a fulfilled life in relationship with God and the people around us; for protection from evil; and to be rescued from our distress. That can also be God's answer to suffering! Sometimes it can be quite liberating to suggest praying with people who have been disappointed in life, praying together for salvation, healing and support. Sometimes people begin to realize that God isn't far away from our distress, but very near.

Jesus' suffering

Even if we know that God can bring good out of evil when we walk with him, and that he has eternity to make it up to us; there's still some suffering that we can't get on top of emotionally. Some human suffering exceeds all bounds: because of the injustice involved when it hits an innocent person; because it's incomprehensible when a life is completely destroyed; or because of the sheer enormity of it. We shouldn't let ourselves be tempted to despair. The Bible itself points out that God's thoughts and

God's actions far exceed our ability to comprehend, and that we should learn to trust him (Isaiah 45:9ff; Job 38–41). However, we're not talking about blind faith here, but about a trust that is grounded in everything else we know about God, in everything that God has already shown us.

The reason why we can trust God, even in the face of things we don't understand, is one of the deepest motifs that we find in the Bible. This fifth motif is that God knows suffering, that he suffers with us. We see that most profoundly in the words of Jesus on the cross, when he who represented God to us called out: "My God, my God, why have you forsaken me?" (Matthew 27:46).

C.: There's a lot I don't understand about God. But when I see Jesus on the cross, I see that God can understand people who suffer, because he knows what suffering is. That's something very special about the Christian faith, that I don't think you find in any other religion. Jesus himself called out, "Why does it have to be like this, God?", but three days later people discovered that God didn't leave Jesus at all: he raised him to life again. It became apparent that through Jesus' dying God was working to conquer suffering and death. I dare to trust a God like that, even though there's a lot I don't understand. If God suffered himself to save me, he won't let me suffer unnecessarily. he knows what we go through. And if God has conquered death, then at least I know that suffering and death don't have the final word.

Which biblical answer comes closest to the heart of the person I'm speaking to?

1. Human beings themselves are responsible for suffering.

2. Suffering shows us what's really important in our lives.

3. When you think about eternal life with God, you see our life on earth in a different light.

4. God answers by showing his goodness in our experiences of salvation, protection and healing.

5. Often we don't understand God, but when we see Jesus' suffering, we know that he holds us safe, and that he has conquered suffering and death.

Our own experiences

Our own experiences can form a bridge between God and the life of the person we're speaking to. When people can't reconcile suffering with the existence of God, our personal testimony can say more than any theoretical exposition. We might be able to share how we have experienced God's presence in our own pain. Sometimes our testimony is that suffering caused us to turn away from God, but looking back we can see that God never let go of us, even when we couldn't or wouldn't hold on to him any more.

When we meet people who have gone through a lot in life, it's good to be modest and not give the impression that we've got a lot of easy answers. We must be careful not to belittle someone else's suffering, or suggest that we or other people are going through something even worse. However, we don't have to have experienced everything before we can talk about it. Even if I personally haven't had much experience, I can refer to the deep suffering of Jesus, or talk about other Christians in our local church or further afield, who have suffered similarly, and pass on their testimony.

> **C.:** *There's so little I can say when I hear what you've been through. I've never experienced such suffering. But I do know that there are people who trusted God and never lost their faith, even when they suffered terrible things. I'm thinking about Corrie ten Boom and her sister Betsie. During the war they were sent to a concentration camp for hiding Jews. Their story was made into a film – you can see how horrible their life there was. At one point Corrie couldn't believe in a good God any more. Then Betsie said: "No pit is too deep but God's love goes even deeper." You can see that when you look at Jesus. God's love was so great that he gave his Son to die on the cross – so even in a concentration camp she could have faith that God's love was with her. Can you imagine that someone could feel like that?*

There's a danger in using your own experiences in conversations. We know how God has walked beside us, so we tend to think that's his normal way of leading people. You sometimes hear Christians say: "I have learned for myself that there's only one answer, that you shouldn't ask for the 'why', but the 'what for' of suffering." Although this response is difficult to put into words that a non-Christian can understand, it's true that it's a valuable point of view, very close to the second of the biblical answers described above. However, if we give the impression that it is the *only* response, we don't do justice to the multitude of answers found in the Bible. One of the others might suit the mindset and current experience of the person we're talking to much better.

Suffering as a starting-point to search for God

There is something odd about this question of why suffering exists. It's a powerful weapon for atheism and it will be used against God again and again, but at the same time for many people this question has been the starting-point of their belief in God. That's why we can try to give the conversation a positive turn by asking them to think further. Let's try to suggest a follow-up to the dialogue above (p.42), in which the non-Christian recognizes that he doesn't really need God.

N.: Now I come to think about it, I suppose I wouldn't like to think there was someone who wanted to interfere with my life and impose all sorts of rules on me. I'm doing pretty well by myself. I like it better like this.

C.: I appreciate your honesty in saying you could easily do without God. If I'm honest as well, I think it's a luxury to say you'd rather live without God, when your life is easy. You don't miss that much. We're talking about suffering. It's suffering that makes it clear to many people that they absolutely can't live without God. It's the suffering I see in the world around me that makes me think how terrible it would be if God didn't exist. Where would I find the courage to live in this world? How would I have any hope? I'm curious about that. Where do you find the courage to live, when you don't believe in God?

We can also ask our conversation partner to be honest in contemplating the suffering in the world. If God didn't exist, and if life simply stopped at death, wouldn't that be unjust? Then suffering would be even more meaningless. It's suffering that makes me scream for God, for his presence, for his salvation, for his future.

Such an apologetic use of suffering must be handled very carefully. People often suggest that faith is a form of wishful thinking. They say that Christians can't handle this harsh world full of suffering, so they invent God and heaven and start believing in it. If it were true that we had no other ground for our faith than our longing, it would indeed be more courageous to face suffering as an invincible reality. Christians do not, however, believe in a different world simply because they long for it, but because the resurrection of Jesus Christ shows them that death does not have the last word. Christians don't just flee the harsh reality of daily life. If you try to handle suffering without Christ, you are denying the reality that has become visible in Jesus, a reality that was powerful enough to crush death.

For that matter, if you look with the eyes of Scripture at the reality of suffering, you will find yet another pointer to God. When people are unable to accept suffering and when they are outraged at injustice, they are reflecting something of God's purpose for the world. Human beings are indignant about evil and long for a better world because they are not made to live in the world as it is now. God intended it so differently. That's why we can use that indignation as a starting-point to refer people to God.

We have good reasons to ask non-believers further questions about their anger at suffering and injustice. Where does it stem from? Many Eastern religions teach that suffering is only a superficial appearance, and if you still worry about it then you have not yet seen the truth. Islam says that everything is preordained by the unfathomable Allah, whose will we must accept. If, on the contrary, there is nothing divine at all, suffering is merely an inevitable side-effect of evolution. It is neither good nor bad, neither just nor unjust. It simply exists; it's our fate, or just bad luck. The fact that we refuse to accept suffering is a sign that the world has a different purpose! It's only in the Bible that you find a vigorous complaint about suffering, because it's the God of the Bible who wants to listen to that complaint.

> *C.: I understand that the suffering in the world really hurts you, that you find injustice abhorrent. I wonder why that is. Once before, you mentioned that as far as you're concerned, the world came into existence purely by chance, and it doesn't have any purpose at all. But if everything is chance, why are you so angry about it? How can it be unjust? It's just part of the world as you see it.*

> *C.: Isn't your sense of injustice actually a sign that in the end you can't live in this world without God? How do you react to that idea?*

How can suffering be a starting-point in a search for God?

1. It shows that we need God.
2. Our indignation is a clue that the world was meant to be different.

Questions for group discussions or personal reflection

1. Have you ever asked yourself why suffering exists? Do you identify particularly with any one of the ways in which this question is asked in this chapter?

2. Which of the five biblical responses appeals most to you? Can you imagine a different answer which might work better for others?

3. Can you name any examples like that of Betsie and Corrie ten Boom (from people you know, from the Bible, or from further afield), that show how a relationship with God helps people to cope with suffering in a positive way?

4. When people mention suffering as something that makes faith difficult or impossible, how could you help them to see that suffering can bring us to God?

5. Discuss a few possibilities for continuing the conversation from which the opening quote of this chapter is taken. What would you want to ask? What would you want to say? Do you think you could express it clearly to someone who is not familiar with church language?

Chapter 4

"Everyone's Entitled to Their Opinion"

The culture of relativism

N.: I've always been impressed that you're so enthusiastic about your beliefs. I can see your faith's really important to you, and I'm happy for you. But it wouldn't work for me. And anyway, everyone has to decide for themselves what's true for them. As long as you respect each other, that's OK.

This could be one of the most frustrating experiences you encounter during your conversations about faith. You've had a deep conversation; the other person has shown real interest in Jesus. And then you hit the statement that brings it all to an abrupt halt. The "in-the-end-everyone-has-to-decide-for-themselves" concept is so deeply embedded in our culture that even Christians are no strangers to it. Perhaps that's the most paralysing part, because we sense that this idea precludes any further conversation: we have to respect other people's freedom, and in the end everyone has to decide for themselves what they believe to be the truth.

In fact the Gospel encourages us to go much further than this, but first, let's try to understand the objection. To do that we will have to look into people's deeper motives and to examine the way in which this paralysing relativism (the idea that everyone's "truth" is equally valid) has developed in our culture. Against that background we can see all the more clearly how different and surprising Jesus is: he is the one who calls himself the Truth in person, and so is also the Way to Life (John 14:6). This chapter contains some difficult concepts, and may demand some perseverance. But I hope you will find it a worthwhile effort to understand the culture we live in, and to see ways of helping others trapped by it.

One aspect of this relativism is the idea that all religions are equally true and valuable, but we will consider that more deeply in Chapter 5. Questions about the relationship between Christianity and other faiths will have to wait until then. Here we are talking about relativism in a broader sense, which not only affects our religious convictions, but permeates all our thinking.

Explicit ideas and hidden assumptions

On the theoretical level, many different ideas can be contained in the statement that we will never agree about truth. Some people say that "truth" exists, but that it can never be known. Others say we should dispense with the whole concept of truth, because there is nothing that is universally true. If you talk about truth, they say, you can only talk about *your* truth: you can't claim that what is true for yourself is equally true for others. Then there is a third group: people who divide reality in two. They have great faith in science and think that with academic thinking we can discover truth, the "objective reality". But with regard to morality and religion, they believe we cannot be sure that anything is real: everyone has their own subjective and personal religious convictions, and we should leave it at that.

However, all these different opinions don't necessarily make any difference in our everyday conversations about the Christian faith. Most people don't have any particular idea about what they think "truth" is. In the main, they just have a vague but persistent feeling that in many areas, especially where we are personally concerned, we will never agree about truth. And that therefore we just shouldn't try.

If we want to engage in a serious conversation about faith, we need to understand the (possibly hidden) personal motives behind these ideas and the different (and sometimes equally hidden) assumptions that are taken for granted in our culture. These are the driving forces behind people's convictions. As we saw in Chapter 2, people are often quite willing to change their ideas and let go of their arguments provided their deeper motives are still given their due. But if these are not openly discussed, the arguments go round in circles; ideas will be exchanged for others all the time, but there won't be any real progress. When we examine them in the context of the Christian faith, we'll see that some of these motives and assumptions retain their validity, but others seem rather less self-evident than they at first appeared.

Not everyone is affected in the same way by the same ideas: to understand them, we need to ask questions and listen intently to the answers. To give us some idea of the directions that such conversations can take, I want to mention four groups of cultural presuppositions that may lie behind relativist attitudes to questions of truth.

We won't be able to work it out anyway

First, there is a profound belief that we have no hope of establishing solid values and ideals, and of coming up with a shared understanding of the purpose for our lives and for society. To understand the source of this belief we have to go back to the beginning of what we might call "modern times". Before then the Bible, as explained by the church, was the foundation of European culture, through which society agreed about moral values and about the purpose for our lives.

Then, as scientific methods of thinking began to develop, people began to demand a foundation for our convictions and culture that was more solidly based and more broadly acceptable than biblical revelation and the tradition of the church. They thought they could find that foundation in the values and truths that human beings could discover autonomously, using their own powers of rational thought. This should therefore be a truth which should be equally accessible and acceptable to every human being, and for that reason it should be a truth that was either purely rational or empirically verifiable. The idea was very appealing: if we no longer needed any help from tradition or revelation, everyone would be able to agree on the values and truths that would guide our society.

This ideal of finding universally acceptable values turned out, however, to be too lofty a goal. It has become clear that we can't discover such truths with our limited human minds. There is nowadays a new pessimism concerning the ability of the human mind to establish universal truths. This results from the discovery that what we consider to be convincingly and self-evidently true is determined largely by our upbringing and by all kinds of psychological, social and cultural influences. Many people have given up hope, not only of ever agreeing with other people over what is truth, but of ever finding for themselves a single all-encompassing perspective from which they can determine their values. Young people in particular have become accustomed to using different values in different areas of their life, even if they contradict each other: with their friends they live for clubbing, at work for their career, with their parents they appreciate their family values, and they may even add some links with the church.

This inability to agree about what is true and valuable has led many people to the conviction that we have to abandon not only the attempt to find it for ourselves, but also the entire ideal of the existence of universal truth and universal values. All people can do is to decide for themselves what is truth, and what they conceive to have the highest value in their lives. There just is no other way.

Everyone makes their own truth

Surprisingly, the realization that we cannot discover the truth ourselves therefore has its root in a more fundamental belief in the autonomy, the independence of humanity, the belief that human beings should be able to discover the truth without help from outside. In that aspiration humanity has been disappointed. However, if people start from a belief in human autonomy, but are disappointed by their inability to discover truth autonomously, they may also begin to consider truth in a completely different way. They suppose that truth is not something we *discover*, but something we *create*. Everyone makes their own truth. Here we see a second way to speak about "having your own truth": not as a disappointment, but as a grand belief in what humankind can achieve in shaping its own world. The root remains the same: the autonomy of humanity.

> *N.: Everyone has to decide for themselves what they believe. I believe that God is love and that after death life continues in a different way. That gives me comfort.*

We should respect each other's views and be tolerant

A third motive which leads people to a relativistic point of view about truth (and particularly religious belief) comes from a proper, but sometimes extreme desire to be tolerant and to respect everyone's individual freedom. This is often connected to negative experiences with real or supposed forms of fundamentalism. We use the label "fundamentalist" not just for certain Christian groups. It may be used for any religious or political movement in which the doctrines of the movement are seen as beyond all criticism. These doctrines may be defended and spread by any means, including violent ones. So we may speak about Islamic or Hindu fundamentalism, and also communist or fascist fundamentalism.

People who dislike fundamentalist movements often adopt the view that all groups who claim to hold a universal truth do so to disguise their own insecurity. They assume that speaking about truth is a form of abuse of power: I say my own convictions are true and that gives me the right to force my own will upon others. However, the general antipathy to fundamentalism and the desire to be tolerant and respect everyone's truth brings a great danger with it. Nowadays you can be called a fundamentalist simply for expressing your conviction that there is a truth that applies to everyone and that this truth is represented by Jesus Christ. Of course, most Christians want to respect the religious beliefs of other people – but they cannot say that it doesn't matter what you believe. It does matter, and Christians believe it would indicate a lack of care for other people if they left everyone to their fate with their personal beliefs.

Indifference

The idea that "everyone has his own truth" can also be connected with a general indifference. Some people just don't like thinking about God and they don't see any point in it. This is reinforced by the general feeling that we can never apprehend truth anyway. Perhaps Pilate's question "What is truth?" was a tired expression of such an indifferent attitude to life (John 18:38). In a situation where people simply aren't interested it's virtually impossible to get them to consider the claims of God's truth on our lives. This indifference is so widespread that we will come back to it in the final chapter of this book.

Four reasons to leave everyone to their own opinions

1. We won't be able to work it out anyway.
2. Everyone makes his or her own truth.
3. We should respect each other and be tolerant.
4. Indifference.

Jesus Christ as the truth

For us as Christians the idea that the truth of the Gospel applies to everyone is a characteristic of our faith that we cannot give up. But we must understand what kind of truth we are talking about here. Otherwise we risk replacing one error with another: we respond to the contemporary rejection of a single truth that applies to everyone, by returning to the concept of truth that characterized the beginning of the modern era, the concept of a truth that the human mind can master autonomously, and that therefore should be measurable and easily accessible. The Russian astronaut who returned from space and announced that "God was not there" demonstrated his own limited perspective rather than a truly scientific attitude. Many people nowadays have rightfully rejected this limited understanding of truth. This can be an important starting-point for engaging in further conversation about the possibility of knowing the truth. To prevent us from the outset from trying to defend an untenable idea of truth, we can observe three characteristics of the biblical understanding of truth.

The truth of the Christian faith is a truth we receive

Christians find it easy to accept that we cannot discover the truth by our own unaided efforts. Such a suggestion implies a gross overestimation of our abilities. No one has ever seen God (John 1:18), and what we know about good and evil shows us that we find it all too easy to adapt what we see as truth to suit our own ends (see Matthew 7:3; Luke 18:9–14). The truths that Christians know about God, about human nature and about good and evil, we know only because God reveals himself, because God makes himself known and because he shares with us his plans for this world. It is not a truth that we discover by ourselves, but a new insight that we receive.

> *C.: Of course, if you look around it's clear that everyone has different ideas about truth. It would be arrogant of me to think I know better than everyone else. But Christians believe that God has shown us who he is by giving us the Bible, and by sending Jesus. That's what we should really talk about: not whether Christians know better than everyone else, but whether there are good reasons to believe that Jesus is who he says he is – that God shows us himself through Jesus.*

The truth of the Christian faith is a person

When we consider the question of whether the truth can actually be known, we get particular help from Jesus. He doesn't only preach the truth, as Buddha, Mohammed and Marx also claimed to do. Rather, he makes a much more radical claim: "I am the truth" (John 14:6). He is the one in whom truth becomes visible, in whom the source of all truth is physically present. That is such an extraordinary statement that there can only be two possible responses: either we ignore it because we believe that the person making it has completely lost sight of reality, or we will have to take it utterly seriously and follow him as the truth. Jesus' life, death and resurrection plead for the latter, as we will see in greater depth in Chapter 7.

> *C.: That's what I find so enormously challenging about Jesus: he says he is the truth. If truth can be present in a person, that tells us a lot about how we can discover what's true. If truth is expressed in words, it's enough to understand and test them — that's how you find out if they're true. But if the truth is a person, you have to meet him in order to see if he's worthy of our confidence. That's why we read the Bible together: it's the way to meet Jesus.*

If Jesus is a person, knowing him isn't primarily about grasping or understanding everything, but it is about trusting him. You can trust someone even if there's a lot you don't know about them. Even after twenty years of marriage, I don't always understand my wife perfectly, but I know her well enough to trust her 100 per cent. We'll return later to the difference between knowing a fact and having confidence in a person, in Chapter 6.

This true God is the Creator of every human

According to the Bible, we meet the truth in the person of Jesus. In that unique person living at one place and moment in history we meet at the same time the Creator of heaven and earth, the Creator of every human. This is why this truth is universally valid: it has meaning for every person, because this truth concerns everyone. When we entrust ourselves to this truth we are not making a completely random and unwarranted choice: Jesus personifies the truth of the Creator of all humankind, and Jesus as a person proves himself to be trustworthy. Moreover, we can go one step further and show that what we get to know here is the truth about who we are as human beings and the purpose for which we have been created. It tells me who I am, deep down, and why I am what I am. That's why it rings true when people hear about it: they recognize it. We discover the lens that brings our lives into focus, as if the pieces of the puzzle of our lives, which previously we could not combine, have all come together.

According to the Bible, the truth is:

1. something we receive as a gift;
2. found in the person of Jesus;
3. true for every human being and therefore recognizable by everyone.

Tensions as bridges to the Gospel

It's clear that the biblical thinking about truth gives us a surprising answer to the contemporary questioning of truth. It is an answer to the disappointment over the inability of humanity to discover truth autonomously. Jesus is not a truth that we can discover by the power of reason alone. He is rather a truth who makes himself known and who is worthy of our confidence.

It doesn't help that the underlying issues concealed in contemporary ideas about truth are seldom experienced as questions, because few people give much thought to truth any more. But it is possible to bring these hidden questions to the surface, and in doing so to draw attention to the radically new point of view that Jesus brings. It can be challenging for people to face the inherent problems and tensions in the modern search for truth and the postmodern abandonment of truth. We can, however, help people face these tensions and problems if we adopt the right attitude, not acting as if we know it all, but getting alongside them, thinking with them, and stimulating their own thinking by asking pertinent questions.

The most important issue is probably the question of whether humanity can truly live without being aware of the truth about good and evil and the meaning of our lives.

C.: I'd like to talk a bit more about this. You say you can't be certain of anything in life. How can you live with that? I don't think I could. Oh, we all have to live with uncertainties. I know a lot of the things I think are important are just the result of my upbringing. But I think it's important that some things go beyond that; some things are true for everyone. What about the massacres in Rwanda? Suppose what people did to each other there wasn't absolutely wrong: instead, that's just my personal opinion. I find that very difficult. Suppose child abuse isn't absolutely wrong, and if we make a law against it we're forcing our personal opinion on other people. Should we allow it? I can't believe that. Deep down in myself I just know that these things are wrong. Objectively I can't prove it, but the Bible tells me that I haven't just made up these ideas. God made me like this. I don't think I could live with it if I didn't believe that. How do you deal with that kind of uncertainty?

The people who pick these questions up first are usually those who can think in the abstract, and look at their own thought processes, but possibly there are more of these people around than we think. The power of such questions lies mainly in the fact that nobody can doubt everything at the same time. There are always some things we feel certain about, even though they can be different for everyone: that my wife loves me, that we should respect our fellow human beings, that disabled people also have a right to life. Doubting everything at the same time is probably something that you only encounter in psychiatric institutions.

When you start considering such ideas you can arouse interest in the Christian perspective. Is there any way of avoiding the choice between trying to discover the truth through your own abilities and giving up the belief in any universal truth? We might agree that the former is impossible, but it seems to me very difficult to live with the latter. So perhaps it's worth considering the idea that we can know the truth, but as a gift we receive from God. When we discussed the Christian answer to suffering, we saw that it responded to our deepest needs, but that this did not mean that it was simply wishful thinking. The same is true here. There are sufficient reasons to be sure that God has indeed made known the truth to us in Jesus. This belief is warranted by his life and resurrection and by the discoveries we make through the light these events shed on our life and the world.

Of course it is possible to doubt everything, but such an attitude isn't necessarily more rational. If people really think they should doubt everything, we can challenge them to doubt their doubt: shouldn't they question whether their doubt might itself be inappropriate? If you can't be sure of anything, then you also can't be sure immediately that Jesus *isn't* the truth. Surely it would be more reasonable and honest to investigate seriously why he claims to be the truth, and whether he gives us good reasons to trust him.

The conversation with people who assume that everyone *makes* his own truth will be a bit different. They do live with a truth, and believe that it is legitimate, because that truth has its source in themselves. Again, we can ask whether it's important to them that some of what they believe is also true for other people. Can we live with the fact that everyone can just make up their own truth? What about the person who decides his calling is to eradicate the Jewish people and complete the Holocaust? Should people make up their own truth about whether racial discrimination is good or bad, about whether I have the right to a fair trial, or whether suspects can be tortured?

The next question we need to ask these people is whether the ability to create our own truth isn't a gross overestimation of human capacities.

C.: Of course some things change because of the way I think about them. For instance, it makes quite a difference whether I'm very self-confident, or whether I think my life is never going to get anywhere. But you can't determine everything just by having certain ideas about it, can you? I'd like to know how you feel about that. You just said you believe life goes on after death, and you find that comforting. But that's a truth you can't just create by thinking it. We'll all discover after death whether it's true or not. Suppose you're just fooling yourself?… I'd rather live with what I know than with my own fantasies. What do you think?

As Christians we wholeheartedly acknowledge that we can't discover the truth by ourselves. We simply don't agree with modern culture that we *should* be able to do so. If people want to do everything by their own efforts, if they even want to create their own truth, then we can suggest examples to show that they're overestimating their own capabilities. People may have to change their attitude to truth. Starting from the Bible, we can go one step further and begin to indicate the necessity for conversion. In the Christian world-view, people's desire to create their own truth and organize the world to their own liking is closely related to sin, and we have to let go of that.

Our attitude: modesty and courage

When we enter a conversation about "everyone has their own opinion", it's not only the attitude of non-Christians that's up for discussion. We've already indicated that one source of this view is an aversion to fundamentalism, a dislike of people who cling rigidly to their personal beliefs in order to disguise their own insecurity. The result is that many people seem positively allergic to certainty, and it may be helpful to look at how we can deal with this. If people are "put off" the idea of certainty by others who radiate a false and forced aura of absolute conviction, we need to have a different attitude: we want to show that it's possible to believe in truth in a different way, that we can face difficult questions honestly and openly. That is why that final little sentence in the last conversation fragment is so important: "What do you think?" It indicates that we are open to other points of view and willing to learn. That's the only way we can expect the other person to be willing to learn from us. It's the only way we can prevent the conversation from becoming one in which we entrench ourselves in opposing positions, trying to catch each other out on weak points. When both conversation partners simply keep putting up their defences higher and higher, no one learns anything.

The alternative is an open attitude in which we really listen to the other person and take their convictions, experiences and questions seriously. This can, however, be rather threatening for Christians at first. We are afraid to face questions, because there's so much we don't know or understand. Yet we don't have to know and understand it all, because the truth is not something that we own, but a person whom we trust.

We want to demonstrate that it's possible to believe in a universal truth without refusing to allow it to be questioned, and to do this we need to adopt a particular attitude. This attitude has two sides: modesty and courage. In the first place we have to be *modest*. There are very many things we don't know or understand. The truth is not something we can possess in its entirety. We ourselves have to listen to Jesus and read the Bible, time and time again, and accept correction. Basically that means that we shouldn't try to hide the fact that we don't have all the answers. It means that sometimes we need to suggest continuing the conversation with other people who know more than we do. It also means that sometimes we must be prepared to find ourselves exploring new ideas and new questions in ways we hadn't expected.

We also need to be *courageous*. We don't own the truth, but Jesus shows us that he really is worthy of our confidence when he says that he is the way, the truth and the life. When we relinquish our own false security we can begin to live in a new joyful security that we receive from God. There are good reasons to trust him, even if there remain things that we will never understand. Who besides him has risen from the dead? Who else has led such an impressive life? Who else can say God himself is present in his life? What other message can reach us in the core of our being and in the depth of our distress? We can be courageous, because we are not talking about our own truth, nor a truth we have discovered or created for ourselves, but a truth that God himself has made known. And again, there are good reasons for that belief. Just look at Jesus to discover them!

It isn't easy to balance these two qualities, modesty and courage. It's easier to be so modest that we lose our courage, or in trying to be courageous to lose our modesty. In practice we'll only be able to find that balance when we ourselves keep growing in faith and trust. In order to grow we need other Christians, so that we can discuss the questions we encounter. And in order to learn more about Jesus and how he relates to our life and our world, we need to study the Bible and read about what other Christians have discovered. Jesus himself gives us reasons to trust him, and we'll be better able to help others if we keep discovering it more and more for ourselves.

Questions for group discussions or personal reflection

1. The "everyone has his own opinion" idea often troubles us as Christians, because we are affected by the culture around us. Which of the four ideas mentioned do you find most powerful? ("We won't be able to work it out anyway"; "Everyone makes their own truth"; freedom and tolerance; indifference.) Why do you experience this as a powerful idea, and how do you deal with it? What answers have you found for yourself?

2. Which elements of the Christian answer developed above do you find most helpful? (The truth as something you receive; the truth as a person; the truth that applies to everyone.) And why?

3. Tolerance and freedom are also important for Christians. How far should we leave each other free to make up our own minds? What is the difference between the Christian view and contemporary ideas about tolerance and freedom?

4. How have you learned for yourself that you can trust Jesus when he says he is the way, the truth and the life? What helped you with that? How might you explain that to someone who did not grow up in a Christian environment?

5. Do you recognize in yourself any tendency to hold on desperately to the Christian faith in the face of uncertainty? Do you try to avoid difficult questions? How do you think that comes across to non-believers? How could you behave differently?

Chapter 5

"Aren't All Religions the Same?"

The uniqueness of Jesus Christ

N.: You shouldn't think I'm not a believer. I do believe in God. But I don't think you should push your faith at other people like you Christians do. Everybody experiences God in their own way. There are so many religions. It only causes wars when people think their religion is best.

Nowadays we meet many followers of other religions who live in this country, and we are confronted via the media with hundreds of millions of others elsewhere in the world. We can see they are people very like us, as convinced of their faith as Christians are, and as devoted to it. The fact that there are so many religions in the world means that for many people it is profoundly counter-intuitive to believe that the Christian faith is the only true religion. It can be valuable to have a religion, they say, but you have to decide for yourself what appeals most to you personally. Every religion has something good. It's both short-sighted and arrogant to believe that Jesus is the only way to God.

This attitude towards different religions is so common in our culture, maybe even among Christians, that it takes courage to contradict it. At the same time such remarks offer an important challenge for apologetic dialogue and a starting-point for further conversation.

Different views

One reason why some encounters never result in a proper conversation is that we lack the courage to contradict each other, especially about the things that "everyone" considers obvious. A real conversation is equally impossible when we have our answers ready-made. Whenever the issue of world religions comes up, we find that people hold a range of opinions, backed by a further wide range of experiences which push them to take up these positions. Before we can reply, we have to ask more questions to discover what we are replying to, or better, whom we are replying to: who is this unique personality, and what motivates them?

People have generally formed a view, more or less consciously, on the subject. Firstly, some people have the idea that all religions are about the same, and that therefore it doesn't really matter what kind of God you believe in. It's useful to realize that such an idea sometimes just springs from a lack of information. Many people have never taken a serious interest in even the rough outlines of the faith of their Christian and Islamic neighbours. They generally know that both have a holy book, and that both believe in one God. With such limited knowledge it's natural that they should think that the Bible and the Koran, Jesus and Mohammed, and the God of Israel and Allah are more or less the same. They then make the assumption that such similarities extend across other religions. You don't find such a lack of information only among non-religious people: you may even encounter it among Christians and Muslims. Not everyone has felt the need or had the opportunity to inform themselves any further – but when you find someone expressing an interest, you have an opportunity to share a little about the differences between the major religions. When you do this, don't make it an academic lecture. It's better to show what our faith means for us personally – for example, explaining how the differences became important to us when we found out more about other religions. Another way to explain is to describe how the Bible itself shows the God of Israel to be different from the gods of the neighbouring countries, and how faith in Jesus Christ stood out in the Roman world, where there were, after all, plenty of other religions.

> **C.:** *I can see why you think all religions are the same. From the outside they do look alike. But when you get to know them you see enormous differences. For instance, Mohammed says that he tells people how God wants them to live. But the Bible says that Jesus isn't just someone who tells us what God wants from us, but someone who actually helps us to live different lives. He's not just a prophet, he's a liberator. That's brilliant, because I find liberation's what I need. I often think I'd like to live my life differently, but I can't do it by myself. Sometimes it's as if you're stuck in the life you're living and you need to be freed from it. Do you ever feel like that?*

The idea that all religions amount to the same thing doesn't only occur among people who are badly informed: even some noted theologians defend this view. This idea is mainly motivated by a desire to look for things that people have in common, which is admirable in itself. Another element is the rather more dubious conviction that all people have natural antennae for the same divine reality.

When someone has the idea that all religions refer to the same divine reality, they usually also have an idea of what that reality looks like: they generally describe this in terms of a sustaining divine ground of being and the ethic of love. There is also a second and probably larger group of people, who say that we simply cannot know what God's reality looks like. They may be aware that, for instance, a Hindu and a Christian have very different images of God, but they believe there's no way we can determine which is true. Some of them therefore conclude that it's better to reject all religion. However, it's increasingly common for people to say (on the basis of the same consideration) that everyone should choose for themselves how they want to be religious. Everyone should look for an image of God that suits them. It's similar to the idea we encountered in the previous chapter about relativism: people shape their own reality and that is a good thing. That's why, even within the church, there's so much talk about "dreams" and "stories" when it comes to faith. Religious belief is seen as the sharing of dreams and stories that give us courage and give meaning to life, but without the need to ask whether or not they are actually true.

Valuable motives

It's striking that the different ideas described above are often supported by the same motivation. Once again, it's important to know why people hold their views, because sometimes they will change their position simply to hold on to their underlying impulse. Perhaps someone originally thought that all religions are the same, but comes to see that this is not the case. However, if he is strongly motivated to reject the concept of one true religion, he will adapt his thinking to draw the conclusion that differences between religions mean that we cannot comprehend divine reality at all. That doesn't bring us any closer to Jesus as the one way to God. So we need to ask questions to understand the deeper motives that lead people to reject the idea of one unique way to God. Those motives may vary considerably.

First, there is an *ethical motive*: people think it's immoral to claim that you've cornered religious truth and deny that others have it. So Christians are often reproached (openly or covertly) for being arrogant. Behind this may lie a strong moral indignation – whether justified or not – provoked by a view held by many Christians: that all non-Christians, without distinction, will suffer eternal pain in hell. It is understandable that people have a strong aversion to such views, especially when they realize that these convictions apply to them, their family and their friends.

Secondly, there is a *social motive*. Differences between religions play an important part in many wars – think of the Middle East and the internal conflicts in Bosnia, Northern Ireland, Indonesia and the north of India. The idea that a single religion could exclusively own the truth is perceived as one of the greatest barriers on the difficult road to world peace.

Thirdly, *religious motives* can play a role. People believe that if there is a God or a divine reality, it should be equally accessible to everyone. They consider it unacceptable that a certain group should have a privileged relationship with God. Another concept under this heading relates to the awareness that God, if he exists, is higher than all our human ideas and concepts, and we can therefore never express in human words who he is. This leads us to admit that people who have a different image of the ineffable divine reality might very well have also captured an aspect of its truth.

These motives are the driving forces behind various concepts of the relationship between different religions, but we can only confront them when they are brought out in the open. Only then can we establish whether these are valid motives and whether the right conclusions have been drawn from them; only then can we redirect or neutralize the influence they exercise. It will become clear in what follows that all these motives, whether they are social, ethical or religious, contain some elements which Christians might acknowledge as valid, but at the same time we would disagree with the conclusions people draw from them.

Motives to reject the uniqueness of Christ	Views that flow from these motives
1 An ethical motive: against arrogance.	a All religions say more or less the same things.
	b All religions say fundamentally the same things.
2 A social motive: against religious war.	c The divine reality is unknowable and religion is without meaning.
3 A religious motive: God is equally accessible to everyone.	d The divine reality is unknowable but religion is a valuable social construct.

However, when people bring up the issue of different religions, their motives are not always noble. Most people know that it's hard for Christians to answer this question in the context of contemporary culture. So, like the question of suffering, it may be used as a "dog's bone question" – a way of expressing indifference – or used to divert attention from deeper personal questions.

A multicultural society

In our ever-shrinking world, where we know more and more about each other, it becomes very difficult for Christians to affirm the uniqueness of Christ. The problems lie not so much in the intellectual arena of theoretical arguments, as in the social arena. Our society strongly opposes the idea of an exclusive religious truth. Sociologists speak about "plausibility structures"

– meaning that within certain social contexts some ideas just seem extremely implausible.

The social reality that makes it so hard to believe in Jesus Christ as the one Lord is our multicultural society. Until the Second World War, Western Europe had a fairly homogeneous culture. However, in the decades after the war people from other parts of the world flooded into Western Europe: ex-soldiers from former colonies, people from overseas territories, and migrant labourers from Africa and Asia. The last few years have also seen increasing movements of refugees from all over the world. Followers of other religions came to live among us, and at the same time modern media brought distant parts of the world much closer to us. Now we call the world a "global village", in which we know everything about each other. Events in India and Iraq appear that same evening on the news in Europe. And we can see from all these reports that people there are as serious about their religion as we are here. We can no longer deny it. The impression we gain from this is that holding on to the Christian faith as the only true religion is simply a sign of arrogance and unwillingness to engage with the wider world. All those other religions simply exist.

The social reality of this encounter with other cultures is expressed on the psychological level as a strong preference for the idea that it doesn't matter which religious convictions you adhere to. All of us, Christians and non-Christians alike, are influenced by this new social context, even if the degree of that influence may vary. We can make our conversations more open if we make that clear: seeing Jesus Christ as the one Lord, and the God of Israel as the one true God, causes certain tensions in our pluralist society. Even though Christians evaluate those tensions differently, that doesn't mean they don't experience them. However, these social and psychological factors are not paramount in the debate over the truth of the Christian conviction concerning Jesus Christ. I want to mention two observations that indicate a need to distinguish between the *difficulty* of belief in the Christian faith as uniquely true and the question whether this conviction is *actually* true.

First of all, it is generally recognized that the Christian faith itself originated in an extremely pluralistic religious culture. In the Roman Empire, where the Gospel was preached in the first centuries of Christian history, the confession that Jesus is the one Lord was presented in opposition to the claims of many other gods and lords. In those days Christians themselves assessed the implications of pluralism very differently from the way many of them do now.

The second observation is that our culture itself is very selective in accepting or rejecting claims to the truth and the superiority of certain cultural convictions. If I say I believe my religious convictions to be true, and that they should be accepted by others, I will immediately be accused of arrogance and intolerance. However, people are happy to accept it if I fiercely defend my opinion about how to deal with the refugee problem or criminality, even if I say that other people's views on these subjects are completely wrong. Christian mission is often dismissed as an expression of a European superiority complex towards other cultures, a form of spiritual colonialism. Yet people consider themselves at liberty to impose Western European economical and political structures on the rest of the world with all the diplomatic and economic means available, and if necessary even by force. The resistance to taking the moral high ground and to claims of universal truth is implemented selectively to say the least.

The place of personal faith

Our religiously versatile world strongly presses the idea on us that religious convictions are not determined by what is or is not true, but by the surroundings in which people live. When you are born in an Islamic country, you grow up as a Muslim. If your cradle stood in a Protestant home, there's a good chance you'll adhere to that tradition, and if you grew up in a secularized environment, the chance of you becoming a Christian will be really small. Many Christians involved in organized evangelism, or who talk to other people about their faith, grew up in strong Christian families. I would like to look briefly at this specific group, for they themselves can easily be used as confirmation of religious relativism.

N.: But you're a Christian just because you've been raised that way. Suppose you'd been born in Pakistan?

Sometimes it gives people who don't believe a sense of paralysis:

N.: I can't believe. I'd like to, but I've just not been brought up like that.

Of course, it's true that many Christians were raised in a Christian environment, and there's a significant chance that we wouldn't be Christians if that were not the case. It is impossible to deny that – and it would also be ungrateful to all the parents who invested so much in their children's Christian upbringing. There's nothing wrong with this: you learn everything because you accept it initially on someone else's authority. That's how you learn not only your own language, but also physics and mathematics, and that fact doesn't diminish the truth of a mathematical conviction one bit.

However, it's vitally important to make a difference between the *causes and occasions* that played a role in someone's formation as Christian, and the *reasons* they have for their faith. Upbringing, social environment and all kinds of other factors play an important role in the fact that people become Christians, but it wouldn't be right if that were the only thing that could be said about their faith. You may be led in a certain direction by your upbringing; worse, you may be pushed in a certain direction; even worse, you may automatically continue in that direction. However, none of this forces you. At a certain point in the development of your faith you decide whether to continue with it. That is part of growing up, and of growing up in faith. Here you are personally faced with the question of the truth of the Christian faith. There may be many factors that cause someone to start believing, and there are definitely plenty of factors that push people to give up the Christian faith. The question, though, is whether one also has *reasons* to believe. In a pluralist culture people may grow up in a Christian environment, but they must have reasons to embrace and say yes to the old confession that Jesus is Lord. Of course, they also need good reasons to let go of that confession!

Sometimes I'm afraid that the faith of many Christians and the disbelief of many who used to be Christians can be described entirely in terms of causes and occasions: a certain upbringing, a certain circle of friends, certain positive or negative experiences with the church. Reasons why we should take one influence seriously and not another hardly play a role. When that is the case, there are a few important consequences. Firstly, it means that people don't take responsibility for their faith convictions: they neither choose their convictions nor hold on to them for any good reasons, but simply because they happened to find themselves with them. In the same way, many others just happened to find themselves without them. Secondly, Christians

84

then have no reason to assume that their convictions are worth more than those of others who have a different history. They can't say that their convictions have meaning for those who don't share their history. Thirdly, such people have deservedly no reply at all to those who say that religious convictions are completely determined by personal history and that therefore everyone should choose their own faith.

Because of this, if people who grew up in a Christian environment want to have meaningful conversations with non-believers, it's vital that they first answer for themselves why they continue in their faith. Belief doesn't necessarily originate in searching for reasons to believe: the initial attraction between a man and a woman may be equally untraceable and not always entirely conscious. But before you get married it's a good idea to think through thoroughly whether you want to share the rest of your life with this person, and whether your feelings have set you on the right track or the wrong one. It's a good idea to ask yourself what reason you have to enter into a lifelong relationship, quite apart from all the causes, occasions and influences that caused you to meet and be attracted to each other. It's very much the same for engaging ourselves with the Christian faith. Our reasons may be extremely varied: connected with our experiences of God, with specific Christians whose lives demonstrate their faith in a convincing way, with insights into our own existence and our encounters with faith. It's characteristic of such reasoning that it helps you to make a responsible choice about the road you're travelling. And up to a point it's possible to share this reasoning with others.

Reasons can be strongly connected to your personal history, to your experiences and to people you have met. However, there's always something that explains what we do with our experiences and why, how we assess them and why. On one day I may feel strongly that God is there, but on another I feel he can't be. There are reasons that go beyond those individual and contradictory experiences, which mean that I assess them differently and don't automatically let the strongest ones define my life. There are also reasons that are less personally coloured and have more to do with insights in the Christian faith, in the reality of God's revelation itself. The questions raised by religious pluralism point us once again to the importance of apologetics, the justification for our faith. It's apologetics that asks for the reasons we have for our faith in Jesus Christ. In the rest of this chapter and in the following two chapters I want to present some aspects of the Christian faith that give us reason to hold on to, confess and preach the uniqueness of Christ.

One way and many religions in the Bible

Israel's God is unique

When we say that the Christian faith is unique and exclusive, we use these expressions to point to several characteristics. We don't only mean that Christianity is different from all other religions and world-views. It is indeed fundamentally different from other visions of God and humanity at certain points, but every religion has something unique in it. Showing that the Christian faith is different is therefore not enough.

When we speak about the uniqueness of the Christian faith, we mean first of all that the Lord God of Israel, the Father of Jesus Christ, is unique. He is the only God and besides him there is no other who can make that claim (see Deuteronomy 6:4). Other gods say the same thing and in that sense the Christian faith is not unique, but when others make that claim it is a lie which needs to be exposed (see Isaiah 44:6–8).

When we speak about the uniqueness of the Christian faith, we also mean that Jesus Christ is the only Lord, who has all power in heaven and on earth (see Matthew 28:18) and that he is the only Saviour, the only way to God (see John 14:6; Acts 4:12). There are others who claim to be Lord and there are others who promise redemption. Confronted with Christ, however, it turns out that they are subordinate to his power and, moreover, that they offer only a new slavery and not the freedom we receive from Christ.

The centrality of this confession

The confession of the uniqueness of the Christian faith is not an idea which is only loosely connected with other Christian convictions, which can therefore be omitted without too much damage. Christianity is characterized at its core by the confession that there is only one God and one Lord. Denying it therefore has consequences for the central Christian convictions about God, about his relationship to the world, about humanity and about redemption. That is why it is not possible to dismiss the idea that Jesus Christ is the only way to God while continuing to consider oneself a Christian in a sense resembling the traditional meaning of the term.

Some suggest avoiding this statement because they think this would make Christianity more readily acceptable in a world with so many religions. Yet when we do that it becomes a different faith, losing the liberating power it has as a pathway opened by God as a radical alternative to mere human religiosity. By giving up its uniqueness, the faith would also lose its persuasiveness and cogency. The central place of that uniqueness becomes clear from five main aspects of the biblical message that all focus on Jesus.

First, the God of Israel is a God who *chooses* or *elects*. He called Abraham, he chose Israel, and Jesus Christ chose twelve apostles and called a congregation. That does not diminish God's compassion for the entire world. He chose Abraham to bless all the nations of the earth through him, he chose Israel to be a light for the nations, and Jesus calls the church in order to make people from all the nations his disciples. God works in this manner because his fellowship with human beings is not the result of centuries of searching on our part, but a merciful gift from God himself, who calls people and who uses them to invite others to be his children and to live with him.

If true religion really had its root in the human search for God, then we would have to say: "We never know for sure how much we are able to know of God; we'll have to value all ideas about God equally, as limited trials", or: "Everyone shapes their own ideas about God and organizes their life accordingly." However, if we believe in a God who seeks people out and makes himself known to them, then that faith can't just be considered as one possible way to God among many other religions. The idea that God seeks us is either impertinent nonsense, or it's truly the only way of understanding who God is, which forces us to assess other religious projects as merely human efforts to find God which are, in the end, unfruitful.

Secondly, as the *Creator* of heaven and earth the God of Israel cannot be equalled by anything in the natural world. That's why he can't be depicted in any way. And because no one can ever see God, he can only be known because he makes himself known, through his prophets and most clearly through his Son (see John 1:18). If God were a part of our reality, then we should all be able to find him with equal ease or difficulty. However, because God is not part of created reality, he can only be found where he has chosen to make himself known. This concept brings with it a radical distinction between those ideas about God that originate in the human mind, and those that are directed to what God has made known of himself. This remains true when we face the fact that in practice we often have to do with hybrid forms of religion, a mixture of what God has shown himself to be and what humans have made of it. The different religions can't just remain side by side as different human approaches to God. God has made himself known and turns out to be different from what most people had imagined or expected him to be.

Thirdly, according to the Bible human beings are *sinners*, and that means they don't seek God, but continually run away from him. If humans do speak about gods, then these are surrogate gods, human projections with which they strive to shut out the true God (see Romans 1:18–23). It is therefore only possible to know God, when God himself breaks through our sinful unwillingness and inability to know him for who he is. The knowledge that he gives us of himself stands opposed to other images of god that people make for themselves. Of course it's true here that the image of the God of Israel is often obscured by all kinds of human sinful interests and resistances, but that does not diminish this fundamental contrast.

Fourthly, Jesus is much more than a prophet or religious genius who tells us about God. In that, he would be equal to other religious leaders and he could be replaced by others. At the most he would differ from other prophets and religious leaders in so far as his message would be more truthful than those of others. Jesus, however, is the Word of God himself, that became flesh (John 1:14); He is *God with us* and God amongst us. If that is true, he is different from all other religious leaders who tell us how they think we should serve God. Jesus not only tells who God is, he shows who God is.

Finally, Jesus not only speaks about God as God with us: he also *reconciles* us to God. In that respect he is totally irreplaceable. Even if all the wise men and great prophets of the different religions could give us a complete image of God, it would be worthless without reconciliation. The gap between God and humanity must also be bridged. The direction of human life, looking away from God rather than towards him, must be changed. To say that other religions are valid alternative ways to bring humanity back to God is an insult to the cross of Christ: it would mean that "Christ died for nothing" (Galatians 2:21). If humanity could come to God in different ways, why would God choose this terrible method to reconcile us to him? If the crucifixion of Christ is central to our faith, that faith cannot be compared with other religious convictions.

These five aspects of Christian belief show us again that a good insight into our own faith is the first step towards giving a good explanation of it to others. We need to understand the connection between the uniqueness of Christ and the entire biblical message. Then we can also explain that the idea that Jesus is the only way to God is really not that strange: it is entirely in keeping with the God whom we know through the Bible. Those different elements can be made comprehensible for non-Christians, because they tell us about the true God who made and knows every human being.

C.: You might say that God can't be known and that no one can know who God really is, but suppose God chose to show certain people who he is. Wouldn't that be possible? If you don't know God it's very difficult to claim that you know what would be impossible for him...

You might say that every human being has some sort of antenna for God, a way to experience the divine. But if you look around you can see that ideas about God are constantly adapted to people's personal needs. You mentioned religious wars. I agree completely: people often use God for their own purposes and do the most horrible things in his name. When we make gods for ourselves they're not trustworthy. Christians believe it was necessary for God to show us in a special way who he is. He did that through Jesus...

You might say there are plenty of gurus in India who have a very deep knowledge of God. But even if their knowledge was right, they admit themselves that they don't have any more than that: insight into who God is. The problem is that it's not enough. We need not only someone who tells us what God is and what God wants, but someone who brings us back to God or who brings God to us. That's exactly what Jesus does...

Five reasons why "being uniquely known through Christ" is an essential characteristic of the God of the Bible

1. He chooses people and is different from the gods whom people choose for themselves.
2. You cannot know this God if he does not make himself known.
3. The gods that people make for themselves reflect their sinful needs.
4. Jesus is not just a human who knows a lot about God, but God himself who lets himself be known.
5. Jesus not only tells us about God, he reconciles us with God.

Different religions in the Bible

We have seen before that in a world with so many religions it seems both unnatural and counter-intuitive to believe in Jesus as the only way to God. Those realities don't seem to go together: when so many people believe so sincerely in other religions, it seems almost absurd to think your own personal faith is better than that of others. Doesn't that just mean you're terribly conceited? However, the tendency to regard all religions as equal is not such an obvious consequence of the multiplicity of religions as it at first seems. When we see religions as purely human projects and projections, then regarding them as equal is a logical consequence. From a faith perspective, however, we look at reality with different eyes: believing leads, after all, to a renewing of our mind (Romans 12:2). We've all had the experience of something that seemed incomprehensible suddenly becoming understandable when we find a new way of looking at it. Sometimes you completely misunderstand the behaviour of a colleague and you end up having a terrible row, but if you get an explanation you begin to view that behaviour in a different light, and it turns out that you can suddenly see things very differently.

When we look at the world with its many religions, it turns out that that world, viewed with the eyes of the Bible, is not strange at all. The Bible assumes that human beings are naturally religious and can recognize certain aspects of God in creation (see Romans 1:18–23), so it's not so strange that religion is such a widespread phenomenon. Of course, the fact that faith is natural doesn't necessarily mean that everyone will be religious: it's also natural for human beings to develop friendships, but not everyone succeeds at it and some people don't even seem to want it. Because something of God becomes visible in creation itself, we can see that aspects of truth will also surface in other religions: they are not all lies or devil-worship. We can learn from the awe that many Muslims feel for the holiness of God; we can learn from the respect for creation found in Hinduism.

The number and diversity of religions are not unexpected when we look at the religious world from a biblical perspective. People continually adapt their image of God to their own personal needs and ideals, and religions are always born within a certain historical situation; together, these facts make that multitude of religions understandable.

The God of the Bible was first recognized by small groups of people: Abraham's clan, the people of Israel, the small band of the earliest followers of Jesus. That may not sit easily with the fundamental conviction that this is the God of the whole universe and all of humanity. Let's try to look at this characteristic of God's work in the world in a different way. God makes himself known in the Bible as a Creator who wants to be known to human beings. He took this so far that in Jesus Christ he became human and therefore *Immanuel* or "God-with-us". God can't come closer to humankind than becoming a human being himself. Incarnation, however, has to happen at a certain moment in a certain place. If God had become human again and again in many different places, as the Hindus believe about divine *avatars*, then he would never have became truly human, for part of being human is the once-only character of our existence, the non-repeatability of our living: we can't re-run our lives, even though we might sometimes wish we could do just that. To be as close to human beings as possible and to be able to redeem humanity, God became a human being in Palestine during the time of Emperor Augustus. But in that event God still had the whole of humanity in view; that much is clear from the commandment to preach the Gospel to all the nations, a commandment which is an integral part of the Gospel.

The particular course that God took for the salvation of humanity shows us that Christianity's relationship with the Jewish faith is very different from its relationship to other religions. For the Jews, the God of the Bible is no stranger, but a God who has already travelled a long distance with them. For Christians, Judaism is like an older brother, with whom we may speak about what we have seen of the Father in Jesus, while knowing that the Father already had a relationship with them, long before the church was born.

When you look with Christian eyes at the multiplicity of different religions, it's no longer surprising that the first Christians were able to present Jesus Christ as the only Lord in the world of the Roman Empire with its many gods and many religions. They encountered all those religions and didn't experience them as a threat: they didn't expect anything different. It was only Christians in Europe who were unaware of the reality of religious pluralism for many centuries, because they lived in a largely Christian culture. Now we have to get used to it all over again. We must learn to see that confessing Jesus Christ as the only way to God is no arrogant belief of stuck-up people unable to see the limitations of their own religious experience. Rather, we're expressing God's graceful revelation of himself and his great plan for the salvation of the world, which Christians humbly and thankfully accept as God's gift.

> ***C.:*** *I get the feeling that the existence of all the different religions makes it inconceivable to you that there's only one true way to God. Is that right?... But can you imagine that it's possible to assess all those faiths in very different ways? Christians believe that humanity was created to live with God. So it doesn't seem strange to us that people make new images of God for themselves all the time. But that doesn't mean that all those ideas about God are equally good. Every culture also has its own ideas about how men and women should treat each other, but that doesn't necessarily mean that all those ideas are equally good, does it?*

Confirmation of the reign of Christ

The confession that there is only one true God and that Jesus Christ is the only Lord, is central in the whole of the biblical message; it can't be surrendered. There will of course be people who say that therefore the Christian faith as a whole should be written off. Nevertheless the New Testament gives us quite a few solid reasons why we should believe what Jesus said: that he and he alone reconciled humanity to God, and that to him and him alone was given all power in heaven and on earth. In the first place there was his resurrection as confirmation of Jesus' claims and mission. "God has raised this Jesus to life, and we are all witnesses of the fact... Therefore let all Israel be assured of this: God has made this Jesus, whom you crucified, both Lord and Christ" (Acts 2:32, 36; see Romans 1:4). In the final chapter we will examine this and other positive reasons to accept Jesus as the only Lord and Redeemer.

Incentives to explore the uniqueness of Christ

Journeying together

We have covered the most important elements that play a role in conversations about Christ and other religions. It's crucial that such conversations don't just remain on the level of exchanging ideas and arguments, but instead become real encounters – not only between the people involved in conversation, but also between those people and the Gospel, and with God himself. In order to facilitate such a true personal encounter, we need to get to know people at a deeper level, by asking questions and discovering what experiences, motivations and reasons cause them to think the way they do. We have to aim for a conversation on that level, because that is where we'll find the deepest reasons for the positions they take up.

You have to indicate that you're truly interested in the other person, not just looking for opportunities to share your own story. That will mostly become clear when you show that you're willing to learn from them, and that willingness needn't be pretence. God's truth is not confined to the Christian faith, even though we believe that this truth shines incomparably more brightly in Christ. When you can truly listen to others, this will in any case create space for sharing your own journey and the role that Jesus Christ and his Gospel played in it.

It's very important that you also rise above your personal history in this conversation about the uniqueness of Christ. That doesn't mean you should detach yourself from it, but in the discussion you have to make it clear that what makes you tick goes beyond your personal interests or those of your friends and family; it's about a universal reality that is equally the reality of your conversation partner. You will have to challenge them to face the claims of Jesus Christ and make it clear that this takes time. It takes time because the Christian faith contrasts so radically with what's now deemed plausible in our culture that it requires a serious effort even to begin looking with Christian eyes at the reality of religious pluralism. After all, a change of insight at this point brings huge changes in how people look at life and the world. If our conversation partners can muster only limited interest in these questions, they should not be tempted to think they know what the Christian faith has to say on the subject. That is often what prevents people from continuing their exploration of the Christian faith: they reject it because they think they know all about it, but they don't.

Given the obstacles we have identified, setting out on this journey requires serious motivation – one which generally should have deeper roots than our conversations by themselves can produce. The motivation may, for instance, lie in disappointment with life as it is now being lived, or in positive experiences with

Christians, or in expectations of Jesus Christ that have been aroused in other ways.

There are also incentives to embark on this journey that are more directly connected with our theme. In the previous chapter we observed that many people are aware at a very fundamental level that complete relativism is not a practicable option. It simply cannot be true that all those different ideas about God are equally true, and that we cannot make any distinction between better and worse, or between more true and less true. We can try to reinforce this awareness by mentioning examples that show how impracticable this approach is.

> **C.:** *Can you really say it doesn't matter whether you're a Christian or a Hindu? As I understand it, mainstream Hinduism says you shouldn't help other people when they suffer, because their suffering is a result of guilt or negative karma built up in previous lives. The Bible encourages us to help other people. And can you really say it doesn't matter whether you're a Buddhist or a Christian? A Buddhist says that the highest purpose of life is to lose your own personality in the divine emptiness of nirvana. But Christians believe in a personal God, who wants to have a personal relationship with you, like a father with a child. With this God you find your destiny as a person.*

Taking valid motives into account

Whatever window of opportunity you find when encouraging people to consider the uniqueness of the Christian faith, that openness can be hugely increased when people feel that their various motives to reject the uniqueness of Christ can be taken seriously. Some of those motives were uncovered earlier in this chapter. Let's consider what they look like from a Christian perspective.

In relation to the *ethical motive* (that it is arrogant to claim that your personal convictions are true), we should recognize that religious arrogance does exist, and it's especially reprehensible when we meet it in Christians. Jesus teaches us humility. That doesn't necessarily mean, however, that having strong religious convictions is always arrogant. We should also remember that people use this criticism very selectively – we've already seen that it's hardly ever used in relation to political convictions and not at all when secular science is on the table.

We may need to be aware of a hidden presupposition behind this charge that claiming to know God is arrogant. Since the rise of modern thought, knowledge has been strongly connected with mastery and power. Knowledge is something you acquire and the more you know, the more power you have over reality; the more power you have over reality, the more you can come to understand it. Modern science is about understanding and mastering the natural world. That is why claims of knowledge beyond what is visible and measurable are easily seen as arrogant. From a Christian point of view, however, the knowledge of God is not something we can acquire by ourselves, but a gift that we receive, because God chose to make himself known to us. That leaves no room for arrogance, but only for humble and thankful acceptance of this gift of knowledge. Instead, it would be arrogant to reject this gift and to think you can do without it. From a Christian perspective, knowledge of God doesn't give you power over God. It's rather God who claims his authority over us.

When we turn to the Christian concept of hell, it's hard to summarize people's objections in a few sentences, but a few indications may help. On the whole, it's good to view critical remarks as positively as possible, and when people reject the idea of hell we can see in that criticism a longing to do justice to the love of God. But it's also important to realize that when we talk about a God of love we don't mean that God is like a sweet old man. God will not allow people who reject his goodness to affect his good creation forever. He is continually working to invite people to accept his love, but there is an end to it, because God takes his own love, and its rejection by human beings, seriously. God's love, however, is the source and ground of our life and if we don't want to accept it, eternal death is the only alternative. C. S. Lewis phrased it very clearly: in the end there will be only two kinds of people. The first group of people says to God, "Your will be done." As for the second group of people, it is God who says to them, "Your will be done", for when they turn their backs on the life and the love God offers, eternal death is the alternative.

Furthermore, we must emphasize that we can never sit in judgment on God's behalf. We must leave it to God to decide who will be lost forever, trusting in his love and justice and counting on the fact that everything may turn out quite differently than we expect. Jesus warned a Jewish city that the day of judgment would be more bearable for the sinful city of Sodom than for Capernaum (Matthew 11:23–24). The crucial question for us is not what God will do with those who reject his love, but what we do with God's love for us.

The *social motive* of wanting to prevent religious tensions and wars is of course very praiseworthy, but the question remains whether religious peace will automatically follow when you abandon the exclusivity of the Christian faith. Tolerance means that you leave others free to hold their own convictions. What if those convictions spur them on to fight others? If you decide every religious conviction is relative, you have no reply to people who believe that their faith requires them to defend it with fire and sword, like many fundamentalist Muslims and

Hindus. You are better placed if you can say that they have misunderstood God: Jesus has shown himself to be a God of peace who conquers opposition by his love, which is willing to suffer for a fallen world.

Two kinds of not-knowing

The *religious motive* emphasizes that we cannot know God and therefore every religion is either equally valuable or equally worthless. It is sometimes possible to break through that relativism by challenging people to know even less than they already do. What I mean by this can be illustrated by a look at two kinds of sceptics from ancient times. Sceptics were philosophers who thought you should doubt everything, but they did it in different ways. The first kind said: "We can't know anything and I'm sure of that." The second kind said: "I think we can't know anything, but I'm not even sure of that." Only the second kind of sceptic is honest enough to really doubt everything. But that means, of course, that they may have to entertain the possibility that at some point they actually *can* know something. In that way you can challenge relativists not to be relativistic in a dogmatic way, but to be equally sceptical of their own personal relativism concerning religious convictions. You can respect them when they believe that we cannot know God, but at the same time ask the question whether or not we should leave the possibility open that God might *let* himself be known by us. If you don't know God, you can't say in advance whether that is possible or not. If you really believe that we humans can't know God, you also can't rule out what he might do – for instance, to choose to show us who he is through Jesus. The only way to discover that is to look attentively at Jesus and ask if Jesus can justifiably say that he shows who God is. This gives us good reasons to start reading the Gospels together and exploring the Christian faith.

The painter and his painting

We have already seen that the idea that God shows himself through Jesus is at odds with the plausibility structure of our society, but we can point to more general experiences that help us clarify the Christian viewpoint. You can use the metaphor of the painter to illustrate that Christian knowledge of God is of a different order than the other images people make of God. Suppose that quite a few of a painter's works are well known. On the basis of those works of art, one can form an opinion about the painter's character and her aims. Yet when several people study her art they can produce very different interpretations. These differences may complement each other, but they may also arise from misunderstandings. We can discuss the validity of the different interpretations by referring to the paintings and asking what makes best sense of them all. The situation changes drastically, however, when the painter herself appears on the stage and says who she is and describes the purpose of her work. Compared to her view, all earlier interpretations of the work are of secondary importance and some debates may even be no longer relevant. Christians believe that in the Scriptures – and especially in Christ – the Creator of the universe has made known who he is and what the purpose of his creation is. In that light all other interpretations are of secondary importance and many efforts at interpretation are no longer relevant. "No one has ever seen God", indeed, but "the only Son, who is at the Father's side, has made him known" (John 1:18).

Questions for group discussions or personal reflection

1. Several different motives have been described which lead people to reject the idea that Jesus is the only way to God. Which of these do you recognize? How do you deal with them?

2. Can you understand how the existence of so many religions makes it difficult for people to believe that Jesus Christ is the only way to God? How do you cope with that yourself?

3. Can you explain in your own words how the Bible views other religions? How might that biblical perspective be of value for non-Christians?

4. Do you think the distinction between causes and reasons to believe is useful? What are the most important *causes* which brought you to faith or helped you continue in it? Can you name *reasons* for doing so, too? Which ones do you think you could share with others, and how?

5. What appeals to you most in the section headed "The centrality of this confession"? Can you explain it in your own words, and perhaps add examples that would help explain this aspect of the Christian faith to people from other religious backgrounds?

6. Suppose you are asked to give a number of reasons why you believe Jesus shows us, as no other prophet or religious leader can do, what God is like. Which ones would you want to mention especially?

Chapter 6

"Just Prove It!"

Belief and knowledge

N.: I really don't understand how Christians can believe that God exists — or that he loves us, or that there's life after death. It's a lovely idea, but I can't believe it without seeing some evidence, and that's impossible.

Early on, in the first week after the resurrection of Jesus, we meet Thomas with his doubt and his demand for proof: "I'll only believe Jesus is risen if I can see him and touch him myself" (see John 20: 24–29). We encounter the same demand today in our conversations with others, and sometimes in the conversation we have with ourselves deep in our hearts. How we would love to see conclusive proof of the existence and power of God! We know Jesus' answer to Thomas: "blessed are those who have not seen and yet have believed" (verse 29). That answer seems to make light of his request, and certainly signifies the limitations of searching for proof. Meanwhile Thomas did receive what he needed: he saw and touched the risen Lord, and his unbelief was overcome.

In this chapter we will try to distinguish when the demand for proof is acceptable, and when it goes against the nature of Christian faith. It's a characteristic of "faith knowledge" that it cannot be proven in the same way as scientific knowledge, but we will see that it's not necessarily less trustworthy. The challenge for us is to make that clear in the context of our contemporary society. In previous chapters we have focused mainly on the obstacles to belief. In this chapter and the following one we'll pay more attention to positive reasons to accept the Christian faith. Why do we consider that we have sufficient reason to trust the God of the Bible and to believe in the risen Lord?

Different backdrops to the question

We have to begin by considering the demand for evidence in itself, because like the other questions we've looked at, it may have different meanings and different origins. It's not our task to provide general answers, but to help the people we're talking to, and accompany them a little further on their life journey, which we hope is a journey towards God. So once again we need to ask further questions in order to find out where they're starting from. In what follows, we'll consider a few elements that often play a background role when people ask for proof.

The broader cultural background to this question is the enormous success of science in modern times, which provokes awe and trust. Faith and religion have been discussed for ever, yet many people never move beyond the level of sharing personal opinions, whereas science, in just a few centuries, has produced a vast body of commonly accepted knowledge. That knowledge has produced impressive results in the shape of modern technology, and its fundamental tenets scarcely require discussion. This confidence in science is the reason why, some years ago, the relationship between faith and science took the central place in apologetic conversations. You could hardly ever talk to a non-Christian without questions about creation and evolution coming up. In more recent years, confidence in science has begun to decline as more negative aspects have become apparent, such as global warming, environmental hazards arising from technological advance, and what people often view as an increasingly bleak and impersonal world. Philosophy has also been busily chewing away at the assumption that science can deliver absolutely trustworthy knowledge. Yet there remains a general impression that science produces more valuable and reliable information than religion. Religious belief is seen as impossible to prove; that's only to be expected, because when people speak about "proof", they're usually thinking of scientific proof.

Starting from this confidence in science, the demand for proof in matters of faith can come with either a negative or a positive intention. It can arise from the assumption that Christianity is a relic from a bygone age, something that people could believe in more primitive times but not today. Like so many other questions, this one may also express reluctance to engage with the Christian faith. However, it may also be asked out of a sincere and proper refusal to take things at face value, and a desire to find good reasons for believing in God and in Jesus. Thomas's question is not unreasonable, and certainly didn't come from a reluctance to accept the resurrection of his Lord.

In both cases there is a danger that we respond too prematurely: "Of course there's no proof – that's why faith is faith", or rather, "But there's plenty of proof for faith – just look at the Bible…" Both answers may be correct, but both require further explanation. In order to give a relevant reply, you need to know what this person means when they ask for "evidence" or "proof".

C.: When you say you can't believe without proof, what do you actually mean? Why is it so important to have proof?

When you probe further at this point, you discover that people have different concepts of evidence, which may be connected in very strange and incoherent ways. Often they have vague and limited ideas of what counts as proof.

N.: When I say I want proof, I mean that you should only believe what you see.

N.: I mean you should be able to provide proper scientific evidence.

Often you find that people have such vague ideas about the word "proof" or similar terms that they can hardly express what it means, but at the same time they are sure that the Christian faith can never be proven. It can therefore be a crucial clarification to ask what kind of proof would be sufficient for them to accept the Christian faith. That's when you discover that they're often making quite unreasonable demands of the Christian faith. Is it sensible to expect to know God and Jesus Christ in the same way as we know the reality around us or the reality we research through science? Sometimes you even have to go a step further and ask:

C.: What if you got the proof you're asking for? Would you believe it then? Be honest.

Some people realize that they still wouldn't believe – and suddenly other, more important obstacles need to be discussed.

N.: No, if I'm honest I still couldn't believe in a God who permits so much suffering in the world.

Or:

N.: *No, I don't believe there is that sort of proof. Religion just isn't something that belongs in this day and age. Most people who've looked into it and found out more have ended up giving up their faith.*

Once again we see how important it is to know what the real obstacles are and to talk about those. It might be the case that the demand for proof isn't important at all, and can be put to one side while entirely different questions are addressed. This shows how much patience you need if you want to engage in true dialogue. Still, you should be grateful for such unexpected turns: they provide an opening for a true conversation. When people begin to expose the real issues they have with the Christian faith, this is an important first step to addressing them.

What you're doing is to make it possible for your conversation partner to understand their own personal questions and deeper objections. In the same way, it can be good to probe further when people say they would believe if only the evidence was produced. Would they be happy to accept Jesus Christ, or would they do it with reluctance? That's how you can discover whether they're emotionally open to the Gospel or whether they're actually very resistant, perhaps because they've had bad experiences in the past. Not all of this is likely to emerge at once, but you should be alert for such sources of resistance so that you can confront them at the right moment.

Variety of proof in daily life

Often it turns out that people have never thought about what they mean when they ask for proof. Or else they're asking for a kind of proof that's completely unsuitable for faith, because they start from a concept that belongs in the physical sciences.

At times like these it's very tempting to score points off the other person, and make them feel you're belittling their arguments. That's counter-productive: it only builds up their reluctance to listen to you. It's better to let the conversation continue and stir up their curiosity and interest. You should always try to pick up on the positive aspects, and at the same time ask what kind of proof would be suitable for assessing the Christian faith.

> **C.:** *You're asking for proof, and I agree. There are so many people who just believe anything, especially about religion. People believe the craziest things about God, about angels, about reincarnation — all sorts of things. Some people seem to think it's enough if you just believe something really strongly. I can't be a Christian like that. If I'm going to trust my life to God, I need to know whether he's trustworthy. There are dozens of gurus who promise us happiness and say they know how it all works. There are so many fairy tales. But the Bible says again and again that we've got good reasons to believe in Jesus Christ, and to trust ourselves to him.*

Many Christians find it strange to talk like this about Jesus Christ and the Bible. As Christians we've become acclimatized to the prevailing view in our culture that you should just believe your faith and accept it without probing any further. It was different for the authors of the Bible. It was obvious to them that they weren't following a fairy tale (2 Peter 1:16), that their faith was about a reality they had seen with their own eyes and felt with their own hands (1 John 1:1), and that people who hadn't been present could fall back on a reliable tradition and on reliable witnesses (1 Corinthians 15:1–3). That's why they were so ready to answer for the hope they had (1 Peter 3:15). So you can be pleased when people ask you for evidence, because it's a reasonable question and it opens up possibilities for further discussion. If they don't ask, taking the conversation further may be much harder, because so many people think that everyone should just believe whatever they want, without having to answer for it.

At the same time you have to view this question critically, because as we have already seen, people are often using a definition of proof that comes from the natural sciences, and God can never comply with that, without being less than God. The concept of proof used in natural science requires you to execute an experiment, in which you manipulate nature in a controlled laboratory situation, and that such an experiment can be repeated. Of course, if you discuss this a little further it becomes clear that most people hold many convictions that fail to fulfil these and other scientific requirements for proof, and that they nevertheless consider reliable.

In a court of law, for example, we may find that there's sufficient proof of an event that cannot be repeated in any way. A murder is committed only once – and we try to avoid similar events. Additionally, in a court of law it's impossible to get absolutely conclusive proof that can never be doubted. There are different interpretations of the burden of proof, as a defence lawyer will try to make clear. Even a confession of guilt can be untrustworthy, perhaps provoked by unreliable interrogation methods. Yet we sometimes find sufficient proof to lock someone away for years. It's just as well that we do, or society would have no way of dealing with crime.

Proof of love is different again. How are the flowers I give to my wife a proof of my love?

C.: We've got different ways of finding out what's reliable in different areas of life. Are there people in your life who you think love you? You might even be certain they love you. How do you know that? What sort of proof do you have?

It's impossible to perform an experiment to find out whether someone loves you. There's no absolutely reliable way to find out, because it's always possible that someone's pretending. Someone who suspects their spouse of infidelity won't be convinced by anything until their confidence is restored. To experience love you need trust, and by definition love can't be manipulated (in the way we can manipulate physical phenomena), because love is free. Yet many people are convinced that they're loved by their family and friends, and they're willing to stake their lives and futures on that conviction. So it's fair enough to ask how they know. The question automatically creates space for a broader analysis of what you accept as reliable knowledge and adequate evidence. There are sad moments when people admit that they don't know for sure whether their partner, their family, or their friends truly love them, or whether those people are pretending, and actually only looking after their own interests. Even then, many people indicate that they're willing to take the risk, even if they're not totally sure, because they know true love is worth the risk.

In the same way, other people take the risk of living with God even when they still have many questions and although, deep down, a sense of uncertainty continues to gnaw at them. They know that the opportunity to live their life with God is worth the risk. If you always play absolutely safe in life, you miss out on the most beautiful things: you wouldn't have the courage to get married, or care for children, or enter into friendships or undertake any new venture.

There's a small group of people who really don't dare entrust themselves to anyone or anything, neither to the people around them nor to God. No evidence will ever be strong enough to convince them – but it's not the evidence that's to blame. It's rather that a fundamental distrust of life has eaten deeply into their hearts, for whatever reason. In those cases it's better not to talk about proof at all. It's more important to address this fundamental lack of confidence: one way is to become a faithful friend yourself, or to help them search for such people. Later on some space might open up in which they learn to trust God in Jesus – who is so much more trustworthy than all those who have harmed or deserted them in the past. Only Jesus can bring true healing in this area.

We can cite the examples of the evidence used in a lawsuit and the proofs we accept for love, and all the other areas of life which lie beyond the limits of the natural sciences, and some people will still say: "There's no proof; you can always doubt the evidence." If people want to use the concept of proof in that restricted way, you can't give them what they want. In fact there's hardly anything in life that's truly beyond any doubt – even science, in the end. All those examples from everyday life make it clear that we often take major steps without conclusive and indubitable evidence, simply because we have seen enough to give us confidence that we're on the right track. What would give us that confidence in relation to God?

Rather than trying to come up with scientific proof for faith in God, it seems to me more helpful, and more in line with the multifaceted and versatile nature of human knowledge, to conclude that there are very different *kinds* of proof and evidence, depending on the type of knowledge in question. Proof in mathematics is different from proof in the courtroom, different again from proof of good behaviour and from a proof of love. The kinds of proof may be different but they are not less valuable, because they work according to the issue in hand. You don't get proof of love by subjecting someone to an exam, or proof of driving proficiency from a hug.

C.: *The question we have to ask ourselves is what kind of proof helps us to believe in God. What proof is in accordance with God's nature, and would be suitable for giving us confidence in him? There's also the question of whether we're really open to him. Do we give God the opportunity to make himself known to us in a way that suits him? Or do we make it impossible for him to give us what we're asking for? God's so different from us, and greater than us. If we want to get to know him, for a start we'll have to give him the opportunity to choose for himself how he wants to make himself known to us. Afterwards we can assess whether that's a trustworthy way.*

Sometimes we behave towards God like some boys with their girlfriends. A boy might think a girl can only prove she loves him by having sex with him. Maybe she does love him, but she might not want to show it in the way he's asking. She may want a relationship, but her priorities are different from his. If the boy's really interested in her he'll listen to what she wants.

How do we know God?

So what is the appropriate way of knowing God, of looking for evidence for his existence and proof of his character? If the Bible is right about the nature of God, then he is the Creator of the universe, and so, by definition, not part of the reality that other sciences examine. You can't measure God and you can't examine him in a laboratory. That doesn't mean, however, that he's not there or that you can't know that he exists. It only means that he is God and, if he is there, entirely different from the created universe. Yet if the universe in which we live doesn't exist by itself, but is made by a Creator, then we can expect it to bear the marks of the Creator's work. These do exist and they're more numerous than we might think. It's worthwhile to look at a few of them.

The order of the world

In the first place, despite all the damage we've done to it, creation displays an awesome beauty and a remarkable order. When they look at flowers, mountains, starry skies and the wonder of human existence, many people are moved to ask where it all comes from. Some come quite quickly to see the work of a Creator. Now, we all know about the theory of evolution. This theory tries to explain things in a different way, by pointing out mechanisms that could have brought about the order in the universe without any external "cause". These processes could eventually have produced a thinking human being. The problem is that while evolutionary theory does adequately *describe* the development of the universe, and life and human existence, that doesn't mean it can also *explain* that development. An explanation of the order would go beyond the limits of natural science. But it seems to me that a naturalist explanation of the amazing order found in the universe remains extremely implausible – except for those who start out with a strong belief that God cannot exist. The question of the source of order and beauty remains as large as life.

This question has been reinforced in the last few decades by the study of the universe from an evolutionist perspective. Scientists describe the so-called "anthropic principle" that points to the anthropocentric character of the universe. By that they mean that the whole of the development of the universe is directed towards human existence. Even if you accept the evolutionists' theory that the universe has existed for billions of years and started with the so-called "Big Bang", it appears that the universe from the very beginning has evolved in a very precise manner to make the development of humans possible billions of years later. If a whole lot of physical ratios in the very beginning had been even slightly different, then the existence of life and human beings would have been impossible. The universe spanning immense space and time seems to exist to make the earth and human life possible. That phenomenon is very hard to explain if you don't believe that the universe was initially set in motion by God with a view to the appearance of humankind. This whole question of the development and the order of the universe could be elaborated much further, but so much is clear: even evolutionists can't just bypass the question of God.

Awareness of good and evil

A second indication of the existence of a Creator who has a plan for his creation is the moral sense that seems virtually universal in human beings. It's a human characteristic that we distinguish between good and evil and disapprove of some things, not because they'd be disadvantageous to us, but because they go against certain moral principles. We think it's wrong to lie to someone who trusts us, we think it's wrong to abuse children, and we consider it morally reprehensible to stand up only for ourselves and never think about other people. If the world wasn't created by God, but was the result of random evolutionary development, it would be unnecessary and even inappropriate to ask whether certain developments and actions were morally good or evil. The only question you can ask in that case is whether they serve your own self-interest and the survival of your genes in a world in which the survival of the fittest is the only end.

In connection with this moral sense we can also point to the value we ascribe to humanity. If the world is the product of nothing but random evolution, human rights have no objective basis, but are founded only on collective agreement. If others choose not to recognize human rights, they're not doing anything essentially reprehensible. Such a relativistic view, however, goes against our fundamental awareness: that people shouldn't torture, oppress, kill, push aside or enslave others. That conflicts with the integrity and the inalienable value they have as fellow human beings. Christians see this awareness as coming from God who values life, because he has a plan for every human being. If there is a God, we can imagine that he might place such a moral awareness in humans, because his purpose for them goes beyond the simple fulfilment of their basic physical needs.

In this respect we should also point out the deep human awareness that there is real unjustifiable evil in the world. As we saw in Chapter 3, that realization would simply be self-deception if there were no God.

Longing for God

Thirdly, we can point out that religious awareness can be found almost universally among humanity. Those who look for nothing beyond the material universe are a small minority in the world in history, and today. What makes people so religious if there is no reality behind it? Humanity seems unable to break free from a longing that continually spurs it on to seek to relate to a divine reality. Isn't it reasonable to suppose that such a desire should be directed towards something real, like other human desires, such as hunger and thirst, sexuality, longing for friendship and for a home? To suggest that this desire has no object at all would make it a strange phenomenon in the whole of the human personality. It's because of this longing for God that many people tend to reject faith as wishful thinking: you believe because you hope it's true. Of course, a lot of wishful thinking happens in life, but in principle, faith in God is no more susceptible to that reproach than denial of God. Disbelief can as easily be the result of wishful thinking: I hope there's no God assessing the way I live my life; I hope there's no God I'm answerable to, who could even punish me; I hope there's no God who knows me through and through, because deep inside there's a lot I'd rather keep hidden.

Jesus Christ

In the world around us we can find quite a few more indications that God exists, and even that he has a special plan for humanity: the human consciousness, the ideas of truth and beauty, the possibility of true love. For Christians, however, despite all the arguments, there's one far more important reason that we believe that God really exists. The fundamental reason why we dare to trust in a Creator who has a plan for humankind is that we know Jesus Christ. We've emphasized several times that if God is so much greater than us, it's up to him to choose how he makes himself known. If the God of the Bible is the true God, then he has chosen to make himself known not only through creation and the human conscience, but primarily in his dealings with the people of Israel and through the Bible in which that history is told. He has let himself be known most clearly in Jesus Christ, in whom God himself has been personally present in human history.

It's not just accidental that God makes himself known like this. It's not only that the knowledge of God which comes from creation and from the human conscience is very limited and leaves many questions unanswered: God could have chosen to reveal himself much more clearly in nature and in the depths of the human heart. However, such a God would still be far removed from the tensions, the struggles and the challenges of everyday human life. God wanted to reveal himself in history because he doesn't want to be known only as the Creator. He also wants to save humanity from everything that keeps it captive. God reveals himself in history, because he wants to give humanity and human beings a new future. God reveals himself in Jesus Christ, his Son, because he longs to let himself be known as a personal God and to enter into a personal relationship with us. Can it get more personal than that? In Jesus, God shared our life, our suffering and our death in order to show that suffering and death affect him most profoundly, and also in order to set us free from it. The God of the Bible is very different from the abstract divine reality that the mystical religious traditions search for in the depths of the human soul. Our God makes himself known in a special way in Israel, in the Bible, and in Jesus Christ. That's not a limitation, but is central to the power and the beauty of the Gospel.

If we leave to God the choice of how to make himself known, that doesn't necessarily have to lead to relativism. It doesn't mean that you have to accept everything that's said about God. A great deal of modern religiosity says that you can experience the divine especially in the depths of your own inner being. We should certainly ask whether that is at all reliable. When the Bible says that God has chosen to make himself known to the world in his dealings with Israel and especially through Jesus Christ, then you can still ask yourself the same question: is that story reliable? Can you really entrust yourself to that? This question will be central to the next chapter.

Some reasons to believe in a God who has a purpose for humanity:

1. The universe has a very particular and beautiful order that is directed towards human existence.

2. Human beings have moral awareness and a concept of human dignity that lifts them above primary urges and needs.

3. Humankind has a deep desire to know God or the divine.

4. God has made himself and his purposes known through his dealings with Israel and through Jesus Christ.

Where does the burden of proof lie?

When we discuss the evidence for the Christian faith, honest conversation is often impeded by a hidden presupposition. Only the Christian faith is in the dock: all other convictions go unchallenged. Some time ago I sat next to a young Australian woman as we travelled by coach from London to Paris. Such a long journey offered an ideal opportunity to talk – at first about the trip, but quickly moving on to deeper matters, about what was important to us, what sustained us in life, and so, inevitably, to religious questions. Sharon thought it was unimaginable that anyone, in a scientific age and with knowledge of the theory of evolution, could believe in a Creator and in Jesus as the Son of God. Later the discussion moved on to the terrible treatment of the original inhabitants of Australia by the white colonists. I asked why this troubled her, since those events fitted so well with her evolutionary world-view that the weak must lose out to the strong. Her striking answer was that she believed the entire world is divine, and that every human deserves respect, because everyone carries the divine spark within him. Along similar lines, she also believed in reincarnation. How could she believe those things in this scientific age?

This is characteristic of our times: people ask Christians to justify their faith, but they themselves hold all sorts of other, sometimes strange, religious convictions that are virtually unjustified and unjustifiable. Part of the reason may be that religious convictions are considered a private matter: you can believe anything you like as long as you don't bother anyone else with your ideas. If only Christians kept their faith to themselves, they'd have no problems at all. However, Christians believe Jesus Christ is not a matter of private belief, but Lord of the whole world and one who has a claim on the people they meet. That's why people demand that Christians come up with proof, and why they don't treat all religious convictions equally.

I can't see that this is fair. Faith is never a completely private matter. Sharon's faith itself led her to think about how she should treat people from different backgrounds, because she believed that everyone has value. Just because other people start from different convictions, she wouldn't accept that they should be allowed, for instance, to exterminate other races because they think they are inferior. Such convictions are not merely private, but relate to the way in which we organize our society. If non-Christians think society should be organized on the basis of human rights and basic moral principles, if they think that certain forms of evil are so terrible that they should be fought, then they must be asked why they hold those convictions.

> *C.: I can see you have very strong moral convictions: you find some things, like torture, absolutely unacceptable. That's great, and it's a view that Christians share. But how do you know there's something like good and evil?*

> *N.: Well, you just know things like that. You don't need proof!*

> *C.: Since you feel like that, I hope you'll be able to go one step further and believe in God. If God doesn't exist, you've got no good reason to believe in good and evil. In that case, the idea that you "just know" might just be self-deception, a by-product of human evolution. Personally I don't believe it is self-deception. But I feel you can only say that if you take this next step and believe that it's God who gives us an awareness of good and evil. What reason do you have for thinking that some things are simply unacceptable?*

There is yet another reason why non-Christians should be

asked to think critically about their religious convictions. Why should they just base their faith on feeling? It's a characteristic of religious convictions that they uphold us and give us strength, for instance in relation to death. Many people today adopt a vague belief in reincarnation as a way to cope with the fact of death. As a Christian you can reasonably ask them why. Why do you believe that death doesn't have the last word? Christians believe this because Jesus Christ has conquered death. This isn't an unsupported fantasy, because we have the biblical witness to Jesus' resurrection. But what basis do other people have for their convictions? Asking these questions makes the point that people make greater demands for proof on the Christian faith than on their own religious convictions. This brings us back to the issue of what kind of proof is needed for religious belief. Once again the demand for evidence gives us the opportunity to demonstrate that the Christian faith speaks of a warranted hope, a solid ground and of evidence for things you do not see (see Hebrews 11:1).

Many strands make a strong rope

There are good reasons to believe in God. Those reasons may not provide evidence as "hard" as that required in mathematics and physics, but it is none the less real. It's the type of evidence appropriate to the specific nature of the Creator. In the next chapter we'll examine more closely the grounds for our faith in the person and resurrection of Jesus as the supreme sign that God exists and of who he is. Once again we'll need to select the type of evidence that suits that specific reality: a historical event that breaks the bounds of what is customary in history, a person who shows he is worthy of our confidence, a proof of God's love. The resurrection and person of Jesus are not the only warrant for belief in the reliability of the God of the Bible. In the history of the church a huge weight of evidence has been seen to confirm the reliability of the Gospel.

For example, the message of the Bible gives a satisfactory explanation of the human condition and a satisfactory answer to the deepest questions of human life. We have already discussed humanity's inherent desire for God, but even that doesn't adequately explain the mystery of our human existence. Human beings have amazing potential to understand and govern the world, to make and experience art, and we have the capacity for love. At the same time there is also a deeply pathetic side to human life. For all our technical ability, we still have no control over our own lives. Even when people acquire more and more material goods, their deepest desires remain unfulfilled. Without God, humans will always find life a mystery, but in the light of the Gospel it becomes meaningful. The Bible tells us that we were created so that we might know God. Created and therefore limited, but nevertheless given awesome potential and responsibilities: knowing God, living in a loving relationship with him and the people around us, and shaping our lives and the world in the context of those relationships. We hear that human beings are sinners, which means that they try to live without God and in doing so they prevent themselves from finding their true destiny in him. And we hear in the Gospel that despite all this, there is hope, because Jesus sets us free from ourselves and brings us back to God.

The reliability of Scripture is also supported by the coherence and wisdom of its message. Christians can point to the way the Old Testament prophecies are fulfilled in the New Testament; to the change in the lives of people who come to know Jesus Christ; to the fact that people are willing to suffer for their faith. They can point to the uniqueness of the Christian message: other religions merely indicate a way of living which humans have to attempt to follow in their own strength, but the God of the Bible comes in person to save people. When we speak about the reliability of God we can always relate our own experiences of our daily walk with him.

There is a multitude of reasons to accept the Gospel. Perhaps, when faced with a single argument, people can easily produce a counter-argument to reject it, because they prefer to continue living without God. However, all those reasons combined are like threads twisted together to form a strong rope. None of the threads by itself would be enough to carry our faith, but together they form a strong cord that's reliable enough for us to entrust ourselves to it in life and death. It's good to point this out. When someone asks me why I have confidence in my wife, he could unpick every individual reason I give and say that it's insufficient, but I know that when all those reasons are put together, I have good grounds for my faith in her love. This is why you can't expect to be able to answer all people's questions in one go – and why you should invite them to continue the conversation. That may mean talking again another day, or pointing them to a church study group designed for enquirers, or offering them relevant books. A relationship leading towards a marriage isn't developed in one day, either, and some people need more time than others.

Our various pieces of evidence for God aren't only like the threads that combine to make a rope. We can also think of them as keys that open the doors to different hearts. Not everyone is convinced by the same reasoning, and other people may not be impressed by things which helped you on your own journey. Everyone is different and is travelling on their own journey with God. We have to discover what moves the person we're talking to, and what will reach them. Some are drawn in by the concept of the order of the universe; others by the universal human desire for God, and others by the moral awareness of humanity. We need to discover how Scripture connects with the life questions being asked by the specific people we encounter and how it relates to the way their life has unfolded. We shouldn't expect too much from abstract arguments that have little to do with people's personal lives; it's better to look for reasons to believe that touch their lives closely. So we need to speak about our faith in a way that brings the conversation back to Jesus over and over again, because he is the centre of our faith and the reason for our existence. He is God's answer to all our questions and the ultimate proof of God's love and power.

Questions for group discussions or personal reflection

1. How would you react to the statement at the beginning of this chapter? Try to list a few possible replies, and then try to imagine how the conversation might continue. Are the different answers equally satisfactory? Why?

2. Do you yourself feel the need for evidence for your faith? How do you deal with that need?

3. Do you ever wonder whether God exists? Can you understand why other people just can't believe it? What signs that God exists are important for you? Do you think non-Christians might find these useful?

4. What is the main reason why people you meet ask for evidence for the Christian faith? How could you find out what lies behind their question?

5. This chapter gives the example of a boy who wants his

girlfriend to sleep with him as proof of her love. Can you think of more examples of unsuitable demands for proof? Which examples indicate that not every kind of evidence is appropriate for establishing knowledge of God?

6. Do you think it's possible to deal with the demand for proof in a positive way, without ending up in a difficult position because the particular proof being requested simply doesn't exist?

Chapter 7

"Why Jesus?"

The reliability of Christ

N.: You shouldn't think I'm not a believer: I do believe in Jesus. He said and did a lot of good things. He was one of the greatest people who ever lived, an example to all of us.

The question of Jesus is at the core of the Christian faith. Everything revolves around him: he is the one who shows us who God is. As Christians we believe that without him we can't come to God or know him. It's because of Jesus we believe that God wants to be our Father and that life is meaningful. He shows us that our search for God isn't just the hopeless cry of humanity in a bare and desolate world, but that God is willing to let himself be found. More than that: God himself is looking for us.

So we're glad when our conversations about God and faith lead us to consider Jesus. If people don't bring up the question of who he is, we would like to bring it up ourselves. All our own questions about faith and the mysteries of life would still be there if we hadn't encountered Jesus for ourselves, and discovered the beginnings of an answer in him. People may ask us a whole range of questions: about different religions, truth, suffering, how we know God, the problem of sin and much more. All of them can be examined in a new light when we consider who Jesus is and what he does for us. That's where we need to go if we don't want to get sidetracked into a maze of directionless conversations.

Discussions about Jesus can often also offer unexpected points of contact, because many people actually do have time for him. Even when they're fed up with the church, even when they think they can live without God, they often continue to consider Jesus to be one of the most impressive people who ever lived. Jesus doesn't let go of people. Let them tell you why they're impressed by him. It may become obvious that the Jesus they approve of is actually a Jesus they've imagined to their own taste, a Jesus who meets their own personal ideals and not the Lord of the Bible – people often have more difficulty with the biblical Lord and Saviour. But their fascination with Jesus is a good start.

What's actually the problem?

Before we try to share who Jesus is and why we can't overlook his importance, we're going to have to listen carefully again. Jesus provokes so many different reactions. People's difficulties and misunderstandings can differ so much that too general an answer can easily fail to touch the reality of their life. I'll mention five common issues that limit people's understanding of Jesus – but there are many more.

First, we must take into account the fact that some people are simply *misinformed*. Before we suspect them of all kinds of deeply hidden aversions, we must ask ourselves whether they actually have any basic knowledge of who Jesus is and what Christians believe about him. People can easily think they know about Jesus because they've heard of him, without ever having read the Bible or a serious book on the subject. Or they have some vague ideas about Jesus but don't necessarily feel very strongly about them – they may not even know where they picked them up. It's important not to attack such mistaken ideas immediately. If you expect resistance, you'll probably evoke it; but if you approach the situation expecting the other person to be open to learning something new about Jesus, you might stir their interest.

Secondly, we should remember that many people are put off by certain *images of Jesus* that they've got from the church itself. For some people it's the pitiful image of Jesus bleeding on the cross, as seen in many Roman Catholic churches. For others it's the "sweet friend of children" from their Sunday-school years, that now seems to have so little to do with the harsh realities of adult life. Others may think of Jesus as the heavenly judge who divides the sheep from the goats, as the bridegroom who mercilessly shut out the girls who came late to the wedding feast, or as the revolutionary who defended the poor. Each image shows one facet of the real Jesus, but manages to distort reality by its one-sidedness. They urgently need correction.

A third issue is that many people have no problem with Jesus as a good man, as an example to us all, as a wise man or even as guru, but Jesus as the Son of God, as our Saviour and Lord – for them that's simply *unimaginable*. Such a Jesus breaks through all their usual frameworks. How can you believe that God became man? That he performed miracles on earth? That he rose from the dead? For a modern person it sounds like a fairy tale, like a story from a bygone era, like superstition. People could believe such things when there was no radio, television or space travel, but not now. Even if they wanted it to be true, it just doesn't fit their image of the world.

Fourthly, when we inquire further, it may turn out that the idea of a Saviour, a Lord who has all power in the universe, is not only unimaginable, but also *unattractive* and *threatening*. Most people like their freedom and want to manage their own affairs. They can accept Jesus as a wise man or an example, because then it's still up to them to decide what they do with his teaching and what they want to learn from it. But they're not waiting for a

Saviour, and certainly not for someone who asks them to follow and obey him. Let's be honest, that's an attitude most of us can sympathize with. With regard to this problem, we should ask the critical question whether people aren't overestimating their own powers when they think they don't need any help. Even in everyday life we can't live without each other, and the richest experiences in life are only possible when we dare to entrust ourselves to others in friendship or in marriage, and when we recognize that there are realities bigger than us. It's the same with God: when you open your life to him, you lose nothing and gain everything. We're liberated when we recognize his rule over us; it's wanting to live without him which enslaves us and makes our world smaller. Our challenge as Christians is to demonstrate, not only with words but in our lives, the freedom that can be found in a life under Jesus' lordship.

Finally, we should take into account the fact that many people have been influenced by a broad shift in religious experience in recent years. In the 1960s and 1970s faith in God came under heavy criticism, but most people could see something worthwhile in Jesus, either as an example, as a revolutionary, or simply as someone who understood the art of living. Nowadays many people who enter the church, youngsters included, are motivated by a more general search for God, or by an experience of God who cares for them as a Father, as a Friend who always welcomes them. Jesus comes into the picture only much later and his role is much less obvious. We're living in a world where spirituality means something once again to a great many people – but they experience God in their own way, and recognize similar experiences in people both inside and outside the church. In such a setting it's difficult to believe that God would reveal himself in a very special and definite way in a small country in the Roman Empire during the days of Emperor Augustus, and that he did it through one person, Jesus of Nazareth. The *one-off, historical* character of Jesus seems to conflict with the universality of the "God experience" and with the belief that God is the God of the whole universe. The earthly character of Jesus seems to contrast with the elevated and spiritual character of religious faith.

We addressed this issue in Chapter 4: we saw the wonder of a God who loves us so much that he wanted to share our human existence; but becoming truly human inevitably means becoming human in one specific time and place in history. The unrepeatable character of his life is inseparably connected with Jesus' being human. The appearances of Hindu gods in human form are not real incarnations, because according to the stories these gods take on and discard human bodies as they wish. The God of the Bible doesn't just wrap himself in a human form as a piece of clothing which can be exchanged at will. He takes on our humanity in order to share himself with us and save us in the process. And just like any other human being, he could not repeat that life.

Many of these problems people have with Jesus can therefore be resolved by clarifying who he really is. At the same time we must realize that some people have difficulty with Jesus not because they fail to understand him, but because they understand him so well. When the rich young man wanted to become a disciple he was asked to give all his possessions to the poor, because they stood between him and Jesus; he went away sadly (Matthew 19:16–22). He understood, but refused to follow Jesus because he wasn't willing to pay the price (see John 6:66–67). There may even be church members who themselves only half understand what living with Jesus means; the only reason they don't leave the church is that they think they can continue their old comfortable lives as well as serving him. If we are determined to convince people to follow Jesus, no matter what, we risk diluting the message: adding water to the wine, or changing the sparkling wine of the Gospel entirely into water. If we ourselves have genuinely met Jesus, in all his radicalism and uniqueness, we won't be surprised that some people don't want to accept his message and his life. But none of this changes our desire to represent Jesus as clearly and attractively as possible.

The Bible in apologetic conversation

When we're talking about Jesus, we can't bypass the Bible. It is, after all, the most important source of our knowledge of him. And we shouldn't be afraid to use Bible passages in a natural manner when we're talking to non-Christians. That makes it clear that we're not just talking about our own ideas, but passing on what we've learned from others. It's also an invitation to read the Bible (especially the Gospels), because that's the best way to meet Jesus.

Still, there's an important misunderstanding about the Bible which can interfere with our discussions about Jesus. I don't mean misunderstandings among non-Christians, but among Christians who like to share their faith. The reasoning goes more or less as follows: "We believe in Jesus because the Bible – the infallible Word of God – tells us about him. So it's no use talking about Jesus if people don't accept the Bible from beginning to end as God's infallible Word." The conversation might go like this:

N.: That's what I find so weird: Christians say Jesus is the Son of God. How can you actually believe that?

C.: It's a good question, but we need to take a step back. We believe it because God tells us about Jesus in the Bible, and the Bible is God's Word, and it's infallible. Let me explain why we believe that.

Approaching the issue of who Jesus is by setting out what we believe about the Bible is an unattractive line of argument. Most non-Christians don't want to discuss the reliability of the Bible; they'd rather talk about questions that affect them directly, like whether death is the end, whether there's a higher power we should obey, whether suffering has the last word. They'll talk more readily about the fascinating personality of Jesus than about the infallibility of the Bible – whether Jericho was really conquered by Joshua or how many angels were seen at Jesus' grave. These are the type of questions which come up when we discuss the infallibility of the Bible. The people who ask "Who did Cain marry?" or "Was Jonah really swallowed by a whale?" are often indicating that they'd rather discuss questions that don't affect them personally. They prefer conversations in which they aren't really engaged. You can make better use of your time by focusing on issues that touch on real life, rather than ones which generate a smokescreen to mask the true, painful questions of life.

Taking people back to the Bible as the starting-point for every Christian belief isn't only unattractive, it will also wear you out very easily. If your belief in Jesus is based only on the fact that a faultless Bible speaks about him, this means that every attack on the Bible is simultaneously an attack on your faith in Jesus. In theory, for you to continue believing in Jesus, you'd have to be able to refute every criticism of the Bible, whether it's the logic of the creation of the sun after the creation of light, the details of the fall of Jericho (about which archaeologists have their doubts), the virgin birth, or all the hundreds of other questions that could be asked.

This is also a reversal of the proper order in our faith. It's the Lord Jesus himself who is primarily worthy of our trust and our dedication. We believe in him because we meet God in him. For me personally the total trustworthiness of the Bible as the

Word of God is of major importance, but I believe in the Bible because it tells me about Christ. Jesus ascribed authority to the Word of God, and so I follow his example; because I trust the God whom Jesus tells me about, I trust that his Word will also be reliable.

It's not necessary to defend the inerrancy of the Bible before you can talk about Jesus. Many people have believed and still believe in Jesus as the Son of God without accepting the infallibility of the Bible. If you want to meet Jesus it's enough to start reading the Bible as you would any other historical work, but with a heart that's open and prepared to meet someone who breaks through all our presuppositions. One frequently heard objection is: "But if I can't trust the Bible about the fall of Jericho, then everything's on wobbly ground. Maybe I can't trust the Bible about the person and resurrection of Jesus, either." That just isn't true. When we read books and meet people we're continually making decisions about what we do, can and don't trust, with good reason. Let people read the Bible in the same way and decide whether it comes across as trustworthy or not. That's sufficient. If they discover that in Jesus they meet a God who conquers death, then Jonah, Jericho and Cain's wife can be dealt with at some other point.

N.: Christians are always talking about the Bible – a beautiful old book full of wisdom. But it's full of fables and legends, too. Do you really believe that Jonah was swallowed by a whale?

C.: Let's just leave Jonah out of it for a moment. Christians don't believe in God because of Jonah, but because of Jesus. I can understand people thinking that the stories about Jesus are a bit like a fairy tale. After all, it says that he's the Son of God and that he came to life again after he died. Even the people in his own day found that pretty hard to believe. They weren't that gullible. Shall I tell you why they were convinced anyway?

Isn't it just unimaginable?

It turns out there are very good reasons to take seriously what the Bible writers tell us about the person and resurrection of Jesus. However, before we consider those aspects in a little more detail, we should examine an important assumption that lurks in the background of every conversation about Jesus and his resurrection. We've already seen that for many people the thought of God becoming human and rising from the dead is unimaginable. That's not so strange: most people's world-view simply has no place for miracles – they find it hard to accept any event that's truly amazing. It's good to bring this difficulty into the open, because otherwise it will always have an effect from behind the scenes anyway. If you're already convinced that it's impossible for Jesus to be the Son of God, or that someone could rise from the dead, then you'll mistrust every witness anyway.

C.: Christians believe Jesus is the Son of God, who lived on earth as a human being. Granted, it's not an everyday story. Could you ever believe it?

N.: No, never. I can't really imagine God, but if he did exist, I can't imagine him becoming human. If he was there, he'd be completely different from humans.

C.: I can see that a God who becomes human doesn't fit the way you view the world. Can you understand, though, that it seems less strange to Christians? We believe God created humans, so he could have made it so that he could become human and still be God...

As humans it's hard for us to say what God can and can't do. When people say it's impossible for God to become human, they're actually showing that they believe they know quite a lot about God. Really, Christians want to leave it to God to decide what he can and can't do. If God is love and loves the people he created, then it's actually very exciting that he might want to live on earth to show us who he is.

This answer makes a conscious effort to avoid entering into a general discussion about what God can and can't do, because we'd have to suggest that our partners in this dialogue are being too narrow-minded. They wouldn't like that, and would probably try to defend themselves. So we just invite them to consider that what seems impossible to them isn't unimaginable for a Christian. We ask them to get alongside Christians and see how they view Jesus, but without asking them to deny their own point of view. They're unlikely to do that anyway, as long as they don't feel there's a good alternative. So that's what we're trying to do: to show that the Christian faith is a sensible alternative and maybe even a better one.

In general it's important to challenge people to hesitate before deciding what is and isn't possible. The following story might help with that:

Long ago, before photography and television were invented, the Netherlands had an ambassador in Thailand. The ambassador had a good relationship with the king and told him a lot about the Netherlands.

Then one day he said, "In winter the water becomes so solid that an elephant could walk on it."

The king was amazed, and said, "Up till now I've always thought you were a reliable man and I've believed what you've told me. I'll never believe you again. You've just been making up stories. Elephants walking on water that's hard – that's impossible!"

Who is Jesus?

Many people have a problem with who Jesus is; they can't place him, and see him as a threat to their peaceful life in which everything has its proper place. Yet, they find themselves in good company. We should make it clear from the start: Jesus can't be fitted into our little boxes. It's not at all obvious who Jesus is. His enemies didn't want to believe in him and his friends hardly understood him. All our questions about Jesus have been asked before. In the Gospels the same question resounds over and over: "Who is this man, really?"

Even in his own time people tried to fit him into various boxes, but it never worked. Was he a rabbi, a Bible teacher? Not merely that, because he spoke with incomparable authority, as if speaking on behalf of God himself (Matthew 7:29). Was he a freedom fighter, like others in those days? No, for though he did announce a new Kingdom, it was one of love and forgiveness (Matthew 5:44). Was he a prophet? Not simply that, for he spoke about the future, but he also said that the day of God's Kingdom had dawned in his work and presence (Matthew 11:27; 12:28). Was he the long-expected Messiah, the Saviour? Even that is not an adequate explanation, because the Messiah was expected to conquer and destroy Israel's enemies. But Jesus allowed himself to suffer, and gave his life for both friends and enemies (Matthew 10:32–33).

It's important to question what we actually need to convey about Jesus in our evangelistic conversations. Later on in the history of the church Christians came to the conclusion that Jesus had two natures, that he was fully God and fully man in one person, without either nature being altered. That seems to be the only way to do justice to the Jesus we encounter in the Gospels. However, we don't need to expect our conversation partners to understand all that in order to become Christians. After all, it was over 400 years before Jesus' followers began to describe his nature in that way, but that didn't stop people entrusting their lives to him before then.

All we need to understand, to entrust ourselves to Jesus, is that he is Lord and Saviour – and in a way that makes him greater than all other so-called lords and saviours. In Jesus, God came into the world in a definitive and all-surpassing way to make himself known and to save us humans. The Bible explains the supremacy of God's presence and action in Jesus in two ways. In the first place, in Jesus the Kingdom of God, the time of salvation, had begun. Secondly, Jesus as the Son of God surpasses everyone else before and after him, because in him God himself is present in a very special way. We need to examine why the first disciples of Jesus and so many generations of believers after them were convinced that Jesus was so special.

Why do Christians believe God was uniquely present in Jesus?

Firstly, Jesus himself clearly believed that something unique was happening through him. What's remarkable is that most of the evidence for this is indirect: Jesus didn't think it was necessary to speak about himself all the time, because his work and his Father would show who he was. This lack of direct statement does not make Jesus' special nature any less real. We see the uniqueness of his ministry and person in several ways:

1. He preached that in his life and work the long-awaited Kingdom of God had dawned (e.g. Luke 4:21; 11:20; Matthew 11:2–15) and that this arrival had to do with his expected death (Luke 22:20).

2. He lived in a unique intimacy with God, whom he called "*Abba*" or "Daddy" (Matthew 11:25), and constantly made a distinction between his own special relationship with God and that of his disciples (Matthew 11:27).

3. He also spoke with a unique authority which was demonstrably greater than that of the rabbis of his time, and which surpassed even the authority of the Old Testament prophets. The prophets said: "This is the word of God, which I have received…" Jesus said: "But I tell you…", as if he spoke directly on behalf of God (Matthew 5:22; 7:29).

4. He bound the people in a very special way to himself. If Jesus had been only a prophet, he would have said: "Repent and believe in God"; instead, he said: "Follow me" (Mark 1:17; 2:14; Matthew 16:23; 28:19). He even said that in the final judgment people's relationship with him would be crucial (Matthew 10:32). For a mere human, that would reveal a grossly inflated ego.

5. Jesus did things that only God could do, such as forgiving sins. Sometimes he did it out in the open (Mark 2:5), but more often covertly, by welcoming people from every level of society in his company, sharing meals with them and showing that even they were invited into the presence of God (Mark 2:16–17). Those around him understood that in doing this he was setting himself up as equal to God (Mark 2:5), and reckoned that this amounted to blasphemy – indeed, if he were not the Son of God, that reproach would be more than justified.

Secondly, Jesus not only claimed that the Kingdom of God was present in him: he also made that Kingdom or reign of God a visible reality, thereby confirming his authority. He did this through his miracles of healing, which were signs that God's healing power was present in him (Mark 2:10–12; Matthew 4:23; 11:2–5; 12:28; John 20:25, 30, 37–38). The most important confirmation of this message was his resurrection from the dead, through which God publicly acknowledged him and confirmed his authority (Acts 2:32, 36; Romans 1:4). The resurrection shows us that the Kingdom of life had indeed arrived. The resurrection is so important that we will return to it in more detail.

The third reason for our belief that God was present in Jesus is the witness of his contemporaries. Apart from Luke, all the authors of the New Testament were Jews, members of the nation who would be the hardest to convince that God could become human. There was no group of people in antiquity so devoted to the concept of God's holiness and the vast separation between God and his creation. If these Jews called Jesus divine, they could do so only because the facts forced them to it! Relevant Bible verses for the divinity of Jesus include: John 1:1; 8:58; 10:30; 17:5; 20:28; Philippians 2:6; Colossians 1:19–20. Neither should we forget that the Bible writers also had indirect ways of indicating that Jesus was divine: Jesus is exalted and worshipped, something which for a Jew was the province of God alone (Philippians 2:10–11; Revelation 5:12); he is seen as the one who gave the Spirit of God to humanity (Acts 2:33; John 16:7); and other tasks are equally attributed to him that only God can do (John 20:31; Colossians 5:15–20). In several Bible verses Jesus is mentioned in one breath with God the Father and the Spirit, and often even between the two, and for a Jew there was no doubt that the Spirit of God was divine (Matthew 28:19; 2 Corinthians 13:13; 1 Peter 1:2).

Our fourth reason for believing in the divinity of Jesus is our knowledge of the many lives that have been transformed through the centuries, from the first disciples to today. Many Christians testify to a change in their life that can't be explained by anything they've simply seen or heard. They have truly experienced a whole new power in their life that changes everything about them, and their friends and families observe it. Of course, there are many other people who call themselves Christians, but who don't change at all, or who even behave in ways Jesus would disapprove of. Some people's resistance to change is not, however, an indication that Jesus can't change people. It just shows that they have chosen to remain in their old ways. The fact remains that the evidence of radically changed lives is a persuasive sign of who Jesus is and what his power can achieve.

Alternative understandings of Jesus

If Jesus truly brings God and God's Kingdom to us, it's not just liberating, but also threatening. He turns all our ideas upside down, with a number of major consequences for our lives. If God reaches out to us, inviting us to acknowledge his reign and to follow Jesus, then quite a lot will have to change. So it's not surprising that people often try to belittle Jesus and to interpret him in their own way, so that he fits better into the world they know, and they can continue living the way they want. However, there aren't very many possible ways to understand Jesus. We will look at the most important and see how they break down as we encounter Jesus in the Bible. It's useful to consider the validity of other options, because it's not only Christians who need to deal with Jesus. Most non-Christians also accept that Jesus is a historical personage, so they can't just discount him. If they don't run away from him, they have to deal with him. We can ask them what they think of Jesus and why.

Wise man?

Many people see Jesus as a wise man and as one of the greatest religious geniuses the world has ever produced. That's understandable when you consider the novelty of the way Jesus shows us God, like the image of the waiting Father in the parable of the lost son. People are impressed with his wisdom when they read the ethical teaching in the Sermon on the Mount, and when they see the amazing way he related to everyone – traitors, prostitutes, lepers, the rich of the country and the spiritual leaders. The idea of Jesus as just a great religious teacher is attractive, because it shows respect without having to acknowledge him as Lord. The problem is that the image of Jesus as no more than a wise man or a great prophet doesn't work if you read the Gospels closely. In general, great religious teachers and wise men point people's attention away from themselves. Buddha said: "Don't expect anything from me, turn inwards." Mohammed said: "There is no other God than Allah; I am only his prophet." But Jesus said: "Follow me, for your eternal destination will depend upon your relationship with me" (Matthew 16:23; 28:19; 10:32).

We've already seen that Jesus not only spoke about God, but showed in all sorts of ways that God was present in a very special way in him. A good, wise man – who is no more than that – wouldn't speak and act like that. Either Jesus is right in what he says, and he's more than a wise religious teacher, or he's wrong – in which case he suffers from megalomania. Usually it's not the great spiritual leaders who point people towards themselves, but rather the bragging dictators.

Myth?

So is Jesus a myth – in the sense that the image of him in the Bible is not based on truth, but is the product of the imagination of his followers? Even the most critical historians don't doubt that Jesus existed. This is not only because the texts of the New Testament were written so soon after the life of Jesus, but also because all kinds of other writers from the same period, who were not from the circle of Jesus' followers, also speak about him: Pliny, Tacitus, Suetonius, Josephus, the Mishnah. So maybe a travelling preacher with the name of Jesus of Nazareth did indeed exist, but perhaps the myth that he was the Son of God came into existence much later. This idea may seem attractive at first, but it doesn't make sense for four reasons.

First, the Gospels don't have the character of mythic text. When you compare the myths and legends of the same period, the Gospels stand out by their sober and realistic character.

> *C.: What strikes me about the stories of Jesus is that they just don't give the impression that they're made up. Of course each Gospel describes him in its own way, but the Jesus you meet is too real to be a fantasy. Not that he's normal, but even his strangeness seems convincing. You keep finding he was different from what the disciples expected – he wasn't how they would have pictured their ideal leader. Jesus keeps catching them on the wrong foot. First they expect a great leader and then he turns out to want to be a servant and to suffer for them. Then, just at the point when they don't expect anything at all, he rises from the dead. You get the impression the Gospel writers still had that same feeling of surprise when they were writing. Jesus seems to be different from their wildest imaginings. Every available frame of reference gets broken when applied to Jesus. These just aren't stories people could have made up, because he's always so different from their expectation.*

Also, the time span between the life of Jesus and the writing of the New Testament is just too short for mythical traditions to grow. A period of at least three or four generations is needed for that, so that the memories of the true historical person can be forgotten. However, the idea of Jesus as the Son of God and as the resurrected Lord is found in the letters of Paul, written about twenty years after his death by a contemporary and fellow countryman of Jesus himself. According to most scholars the oldest Gospel, that of Mark, was written around thirty or forty years after Jesus' death by someone who had known him personally.

If there had been a process of myth formation to make Jesus of Nazareth appear divine, you'd expect to be able to detect two distinct layers in the stories and traditions about him: an older layer about a prophet or travelling preacher, and a younger layer in which he develops divine characteristics. Of course it's possible that there has been development in the stories about Jesus passed down to us. It's even probable, because the Gospels clearly show that the disciples scarcely understood him at first, and it was only after the resurrection and the gift of the Holy Spirit that they really began to grasp who he truly was. Because all the New Testament texts were written after the resurrection, it's only to be expected that the stories they tell are interpreted in the light of the writers' subsequent understanding. You get that impression most of all from John's Gospel. But that doesn't mean that at first Jesus was spoken of as a normal human being. Even in the very oldest parts of the New Testament we encounter a Jesus who doesn't fit the image of a mere mortal, not even of a person with miraculous and other divine gifts. I've indicated this in the depictions of Jesus I've mentioned above, by mainly using Bible verses that even critical Bible scholars consider to originate with Jesus or the first disciples. The development of the tradition behind the New Testament is not one of the deification of a merely human Jesus, but of growing insight into what at first was not fully understood.

Finally we must remember that most writers of the New Testament were Jews, who knew perfectly well that God was essentially different from human beings; they were the last people to want to make humans into gods. The fact that in the end these Jews saw Jesus as divine can only mean that the reality they encountered in him forced them to do so.

Guru?

New Age thinking describes Jesus as a guru. That would mean that the New Testament stories were about someone who was said to be divine, but not in a way that made him decisively different from other people. A guru points people inward to discover and set free their own inner divine being. If you consider Jesus in the terms of Eastern religions such as Hinduism and Buddhism, you might be able to depict him in that way. The problem is that Jesus was not a Hindu or Buddhist, but a Jew. He had a radically different view of reality from the Eastern religions, in which all reality shares in the divine. For Jesus there was a precise and fundamental distinction between God the Creator and his creations, the world and humanity. Anyway, if Jesus was trying to teach like a guru, how the divine in each person could come to full development and be set free from earthly shackles, then he failed completely: His disciples and later followers all held to that radical Jewish distinction between God and creation, and the non-divine nature of human beings. They didn't expect humanity to be set free from this physical and earthly life; rather they hoped for the resurrection of the body.

Simply wrong?

There is only one other possibility left. Perhaps Jesus was just plain wrong. Perhaps it just wasn't true when he claimed that the Kingdom of God had come in him. Yet we can also rule out the idea that he was deluded, a liar or a psychiatric patient. Of course there are people who gather supporters around them by saying they can save the world, and in psychiatric institutions you can find people who think they're God. But everything else we know about Jesus conflicts with that idea. He wasn't a liar but truth itself, willing to suffer and face death for his convictions. You don't do that for a lie. His message and ministry didn't bring him any advantage. He wasn't a weak or unstable personality whom people looked at with pity: instead, they stood in awe of his deep wisdom and sharp insight. Was he perhaps just led astray by his upbringing and his environment, by his own faith development? But if his environment had shaped him, he would be more likely to assume the role of revolutionary liberator taking the lead in a freedom fight. The pressure to take on that role is continually visible in Jesus' history, and it's equally clear that he resisted it, just as he rejected all the images that people had of him. He turned out to be different all the time. He also had a sharp eye for self-deception in the people he encountered, such as the scribes. It would be strange to suggest that such a person would not be able to see through his own self-delusion.

The most important reason to discard the idea that Jesus was self-deceived, a liar or mentally ill, is that people said he was raised from the dead. If that is true, then God has confirmed his life and work, something unimaginable otherwise. The resurrection of Jesus is also the most important reason to reject the idea that he was just a religious teacher or a myth. Jesus shows us that the power of the Kingdom he announced and embodied was stronger than death. The physical resurrection also disqualifies him as an Eastern guru, who should be setting an example of how to escape earthly life. We can understand that modern people find it hard to believe that Jesus is the Son of God: it just doesn't fit the image we have of the world. But the reality of Jesus himself forces us to do so. It turns out there are not many other possibilities and they all demand even more faith: faith in a wise man who grossly overestimated himself, in a myth shaped by Jews who themselves had known Jesus, in a Jewish guru, in a failed preacher who rose from the dead. Those alternatives prove implausible for a range of reasons. Most significant of them is the resurrection, which disqualifies them all.

Alternative views of Jesus
and reasons why they don't do justice to history

He was a wise man	The significance he attributed to himself; his resurrection.
He was a myth	The realistic character of the stories; the short time between Jesus' life and the writing of the Gospels; the lack of an older layer in the stories about a normal human Jesus; the writers being Jewish; his resurrection.
He was a guru	His Jewish view of reality; the content of his teaching; the effect of his teaching; his resurrection.
He was wrong	His character; his resurrection.

The resurrection of Jesus

In the New Testament faith in the resurrection is central to the hope we have as Christians (1 Corinthians 15:1–14) and also to the discovery of who Jesus really is. Jesus' followers believed that God had truly made himself known in Jesus Christ, and had intervened and conquered death, because they had seen how Jesus was raised from the dead (Acts 2:32, 36; Romans 1:4). In this event God had decisively confirmed what Jesus said of himself. That's why there's so much emphasis in the New Testament on the reliability of the witnesses to the resurrection (1 Corinthians 15:1–3; Matthew 28; etc.).

Over the centuries since then people have looked at the testimonies to the resurrection with the eyes of a lawyer, judge, historian, or journalist and concluded that they are reliable. A famous example is the journalist Frank Morison who set out to write a book explaining that Jesus didn't actually rise from the dead. His research forced him to change his opinion and the resulting book, *Who Moved the Stone?*, ends up defending the reliability of the biblical testimonies to the resurrection! Let's look at a few of the most important reasons for considering that witness to be reliable:

1. The grave was empty. Shortly after the death of Jesus his disciples proclaimed in Jerusalem that Jesus had risen. That would be ridiculous if he were still buried there. The opponents of the disciples, the Jewish leaders or the Roman authorities, would have needed only to point out the presence of the grave. We know they tried to make people believe that the disciples had stolen the body (Matthew 28:11–15), but they never tried to suggest that the dead body was still there or that the grave could not be found. They were unable to deny that the grave was empty.

2. Many people saw the risen Lord. Even years later, people could be referred to those witnesses (1 Corinthians 15:1– 8).

3. Many disciples subsequently sealed their faith in the resurrection of the Lord Jesus by their death as martyrs. Only a few people are willing to die for the truth; no one is willing to die for a lie.

4. The continuing existence of the church is a visible consequence of Jesus' resurrection: how could it be that the small group of disciples of Jesus of Nazareth, who after his crucifixion were completely defeated and hopeless, became the founders of a new community that proclaimed that their Lord was still alive? That was only possible because the risen Lord himself brought them out of that situation of utter despair and defeat.

5. The testimonies to the resurrection in the last chapters of the Gospels have the character of texts that reflect a reality that was experienced but partly uncomprehended, rather than of made-up stories. For instance, the first witnesses to the resurrection were women. No one would invent such a detail in a culture in which women carry little value as witnesses. Similarly, the

description of Jesus who is at first unrecognizable, and can enter through closed doors, but at the same time is able to eat (Luke 24:36, 42), reflects the surprise and amazement of the disciples, rather than a story that was made up to human requirements.

6. There are still testimonies of people who have met the risen Lord Jesus, for instance from Islamic countries, and there are many more who experience his strength and personal presence in their lives.

Of course, many people deny that the reasons mentioned here are sufficient to accept the reality of the resurrection, but are there any more credible alternatives? Let us consider five alternative interpretations that have been proposed.

The theory that Jesus wasn't fully dead, but *only unconscious*, is the one we should take least seriously. The people who crucified him were professionals and they could be relied on to check that death had occurred (John 19:33–34). At the time, nobody doubted that Jesus had really died. It's equally unimaginable that a weakened and half-dead Jesus could have had the strength to roll away the stone in front of the grave, and then convince his disciples that he had conquered death. In any case, why would anyone with his character want to perpetrate such a lie?

The rumour spread by the leaders of the Jewish people, that the disciples had *stolen the body*, is equally unconvincing because of what we know about the disciples: on the one hand their fear and dismay after Jesus' death, and on the other hand their courage, and their willingness to die for their faith after the resurrection.

The idea that the resurrection is a *myth* that developed in the years after Jesus' death breaks down for the same reasons as the suggestion that Jesus' divinity was a myth. In 1 Corinthians 15:1–3 we read that Paul heard the story several years after Christ's death: the account has a realistic and non-mythical character and there are no traces of older stories of a Jesus who had not really risen. For Paul and the other authors of the New Testament it was no myth: they wrote that the resurrection had really happened and they knew it. If they were proclaiming something they knew to be a myth as reality, it would be nothing more than a lie.

Could the disciples simply have been misled: were the appearances of Jesus merely *hallucinations*? That interpretation conflicts with the fact of the empty grave, and also with the fact that none of the disciples suggested that the appearances were anything other than reality. When I don't believe someone, I might say that I don't trust him and that he has made the story up, but I'd have no reason to suggest that he is hallucinating. It would be difficult to attribute hallucinations to the first followers of Jesus without indicating that there were psychological or psychiatric causes. The disciples had no expectation that Jesus would rise from the dead because they knew all too well that he had died a horrible death. The people who first spoke about his resurrection were looked at doubtfully (Luke 24:22–24; John 20:25). Jesus' appearances to the disciples at first evoked disbelief (Luke 24:37, 41; Matthew 28:17). Paul even mentions an appearance to James, a later son of Mary and therefore a half-brother of Jesus (1 Corinthians 15:7), who hadn't previously believed in Jesus, but who took up an important place in the fellowship after the resurrection. Finally, hallucinations are individual events. They can't explain the events in the stories in the Gospels and elsewhere of Jesus appearing to groups of disciples and even to hundreds of followers at the same time (1 Corinthians 15:5–6).

So were the experiences of the risen Lord *visions*, instead, as some theologians claim? The difference between a hallucination and a vision is that the first is deceptive and comes from the subconscious, while the second comes from God – that, at any rate, is what the Bible writers assumed. The problem with this is that the Bible writers were much more familiar with the idea of visions than we are. Paul had experienced a vision himself (2 Corinthians 12:1–5). However, the appearances of Jesus were described not as visions, but as an objective reality, as if the disciples truly met the risen Lord in his renewed bodily existence. If such visions came from God, it's difficult to imagine that they could be misleading. If they didn't come from God, we fall back on the hallucination theory. In both cases, of course, the reality of the empty grave remains an inexplicable fact. If God didn't resurrect Jesus of Nazareth, why would there be an empty grave, and why would he send such a vision? If he did resurrect him, why would Jesus be seen in a vision but not in reality?

Just as when we considered our faith in the person of Jesus, it turns out that greater faith is needed to cling to the idea that Jesus didn't rise from the dead, than to believe that he did. Can you believe in a God who sends misleading visions, or that hundreds of people experienced simultaneous hallucinations for no reason? Can you believe that someone invented the story of the empty grave, even though it would be so easy for the authorities to check it? And can you believe that the disciples became the courageous heralds of their faith, and martyrs for the resurrection, if the final sight they had of Jesus really was his death?

What are the most important reasons for faith in Jesus?

1. The crucial meaning that Jesus gave to his own person and work.

2. His character and actions.

3. The conviction of his followers.

4. His resurrection from the dead.

5. All alternative explanations turn out to be unsatisfactory.

6. His influence in changing human lives.

Meeting Jesus

In the previous chapter we pointed out that every reality requires its own kind of proof. Physical evidence differs from legal evidence and that again from the evidence of love. The same is true when we consider Jesus. Since he lived two thousand years ago, our knowledge of him relies on contemporary accounts. That's why we've focused mostly on historical arguments and on the reliability of the witnesses to his life and resurrection. This is typical of any critical study of something that happened in the past: we have, as it were, summoned the writers of the New Testament to court, and we've discovered that their testimony is reliable.

It's less common to summon a person before a judge – you do that only when you have major problems with trusting them. The normal process and more respectful way of getting to know someone is to spend time together and get acquainted. The usual way to find out if witnesses are reliable is also through personal contact or reading their testimonies. So when discussing whether Jesus and the testimonies about him are reliable, you will also have to invite people to read the Gospels for themselves – either alone or in a group. Obviously the best place is in a church setting where believers and non-believers can study and share their insights together.

When you begin reading the Gospels, you discover an honest and reliable testimony, and meet a person full of integrity. Some people try to pass themselves off as something other than their real selves, but not Jesus. In the end he was crucified because people couldn't accept what he said he was. In Jesus, you don't meet any kind of manipulative personality: he was just as he was and he left it up to people to accept him or not (John 6: 66–67).

When we invite people to meet Jesus personally and get to know him, we can even go a step further. The resurrection of Jesus is not only an event in the past, but something that touches us now, directly. Jesus is alive today! He is still the one to whom God has given all power on earth and in the universe and he is the one who wants to be our Saviour, our Lord and our Friend. There may be an appropriate moment when we can invite people to pray in order to meet him, either alone or with us. That prayer will differ according to the personal journeys of the people praying. If we have the opportunity to lead a prayer, we can sometimes put people's real pain, difficulties and doubts before God. Even when people aren't yet ready to pray themselves, they often appreciate it when we pray on their behalf. We can also invite them to express their desire to meet Jesus and their willingness to listen. Sometimes they will have travelled far enough on their journey to God that they are ready to entrust their life to Jesus.

If your ongoing friendship has developed well, an invitation to prayer won't change the tone of the conversation too much. If conversations are conducted thoughtfully and sensitively, the whole encounter should have the character of an invitation rather than a dispute. And if all goes well we should have ended up time and time again with Jesus, because he is the one the conversation is all about. When you finally reach the point of praying together you have taken a wonderful step forward and opened yourselves to an awesome grace, because then God becomes the third person in the conversation – or rather the first – and God is a good listener, better than we will ever be.

Questions for group discussions or personal reflection

1. Do you know people who find it hard to believe the Bible? Do you sometimes find it hard yourself? How do you deal with it? What do you think of the way the problem is addressed in this chapter?

2. Just like the idea that God could become human, for many non-Christians the idea that Jesus could rise from the dead seems impossible and unimaginable. How might you explain the different view that Christians take? How does our perspective on reality change when we know God and we understand who Jesus is?

3. The section headed "Who is Jesus?" includes some specifically Christian terminology. It's important to remember that these terms can be confusing for non-Christians. How would they interpret the expression "the Kingdom of God"? How could you explain the idea that "in Jesus the Kingdom of God has dawned"?

4. What do you personally consider the most important reasons for trusting Jesus? Could you make those reasons clear to non-Christians? Which of the reasons mentioned in this chapter do you think are most convincing for non-Christians and why?

5. How important is it to you that the accounts of the resurrection of Jesus are reliable? Why?

6. How could you help people discover that it's possible to meet Jesus today?

Chapter 8

"Why Bother?"

Responding to religious indifference

N.: My life's just fine. Nice job, great partner. There have always been problems in the world, and there always will be, whatever I do. Don't talk to me about religion. I can manage my own life.

In previous chapters we've looked at a number of critical reactions to the Christian faith. A bigger problem, however, is that many people don't have any reaction at all when they hear about Jesus. They can't be bothered, one way or the other. So they don't ask any questions. It's as if someone asked you to become a member of the Society for the Improvement of the Colourfastness of Tibetan Robins – why would it interest you? Many people see the Christian message as completely off the wall, and if they respond at all it's out of politeness.

All of us consider certain convictions to be irrational. Prince Charles' enthusiasm for complementary medicine, for example, is not shared by everyone. But all of us can understand that people with chronic or incurable diseases are desperately looking for healing. That's why the debate in the media about these matters is so passionate. However, for many people today the Christian faith is not only irrational, but utterly irrelevant. "What difference does it make?" The question expresses a lack of motivation to ask real questions. They're just not interested.

Some Christians find it difficult to understand this

attitude. They feel in the depths of their being that their entire life depends on their relationship with God. Indifference is so incomprehensible to them that they can't see how to bridge the gap and make any sort of contact.

Indifference has always been around. Pilate's question "What is truth?" sounds more like a reluctance to question the situation closely than an expression of genuine interest. But the extent of the modern tendency to religious indifference is new in world history. In the West (and in other parts of the world under Western influence) religious indifference has attained unequalled influence. It's so characteristic of our culture that many Christians sympathize with it – they are, after all, part of the modern world. They sometimes feel just as strongly how weird and improbable their faith can appear.

If we want to understand today's religious indifference, we need to consider the factors that contributed to its development.

A culture of indifference

Religious indifference is primarily a consequence of the profound influence of science. From the time we start school, our perception of reality is informed by a perspective in which there is no place for God, miracles, and a life after death. In the past, people still heard the voice of God in the thunder or saw war and famine as a sign that the end of the world was near. Now we can explain almost anything. Anything we can't yet explain will doubtless be better understood in the future. Of course, Christians believe that faith and science, properly understood, don't have to exclude each other, but in most people's experience they do. I deliberately say "in most people's experience", because this goes far beyond what they actually *believe* about science. At a basic level, most people *live* as if there's nothing more to life than what they can see and touch. Many no longer have any perception of anything remotely spiritual.

Our culture is also increasingly materialist, and not only in the sense that people believe there's nothing more to life than the physical world. Their values are materialist, too: when you ask what people value most (and when you look at what they actually invest in), it's clear that material well-being is high on the agenda. Health is important, but it's primarily understood as physical (or possibly psychological) health, not spiritual. The media of course play an important role in this. Television, the Internet, radio and the printed press are mainly financed by advertising, so we're flooded with commercials and programmes telling us openly or implying that our lives are successful and fulfilled only when we're good consumers.

A third factor contributing to widespread religious indifference is contemporary pragmatism. Our culture shows little interest in what is true and good, but rather in what "works". This is evident when we consider which professions are most highly valued (and highly paid) in our society. In the past the most valued professions would have been the military, for defending the honour of the country, or philosophy, for reflecting on what is true and good, or science, for the search for knowledge. In contemporary society, on the other hand, the best-paying jobs are those of the manager, the therapist, the footballer and the showbiz entertainer. All these professions are characterized by their lack of interest in what is true and good and their corresponding concentration on what works. "All I want is to be happy" is a cry we often hear. But we need to realize that this contemporary quest for happiness is far removed from the long history of philosophical reflection on the nature of true happiness. In many cases, life today is centred on what makes people comfortable and gives them a buzz. Once people begin to go beyond those feelings and ask what really brings us true happiness, they have already taken a giant step forward.

These three central cultural traits – scientism, materialism and pragmatism – are so pervasive that most people don't see how strange it is to experience reality and live in this stunted way. It's vital for Christians to realize how weirdly twenty-first-century Westerners are wired.

Indifferent people

In all dialogue about faith we're responding not only to an indifferent culture, but also to the individuals who participate in this culture in various ways. We need to understand that people change. Some may once have been actively engaged with the church or with religion in general, but later their interest cooled. This may be the result of specific disappointments with the church, with Christians, or with other religious people. They may also have gradually become more preoccupied with other matters so that faith, or an interest in faith, slowly withers. "The worries of this life and the deceitfulness of wealth choke [the word]", as Jesus himself notes (Matthew 13:22). A middle-aged man once expressed it in this way:

> I was always a real seeker. Maybe it was the atmosphere:
> late sixties, flower power, you know. I went to India, looking
> for a personal guru, seeking spiritual renewal, and so on. To
> be honest, I didn't find anything. Lot of hot air. The whole
> thing was a disappointment. Here in the West it's even more
> of a spiritual desert. I think I've given up hope now... Over
> the years I've shed a lot of illusions and become much more
> rational.[2]

But it can also happen the other way round. For the new generation growing up in the West, an evolutionist understanding of the world and a materialist view of life is self-evident. They'll experience life only within those narrow parameters unless they are forcefully roused. Moreover, many young adults are so busy with their daily lives, making a career, looking for a partner, starting a family, that this demands all their attention.

Sometimes we may need to accept that some people, at certain stages of their life, are just not interested in talking about faith. Their life runs smoothly or trudges along, but it never gives them cause to reflect seriously on the question of what makes it worth living. The only thing we can do in that case is avoid being too pushy now, and thus creating barriers to future conversation. We can try to remain welcoming and accessible should a new opening arise. That may come when their life takes a new turn, such as the birth of a first baby, or when their lifestyle is radically shaken by some external event. No life continues carefree for ever.

Finally, we need to realize that not everyone is as indifferent to God as they may appear. Perhaps they think they've found the answer in some other religion or spirituality. Perhaps they think they can retain the essence of the Christian faith in some other way: "I try to be a good person, so why do I need the church?" These attitudes demonstrate the need for attentive listening on our part: where does their indifference come from? How deep are its roots?

The relevance of the Christian faith

The Bible is familiar with the question of whether faith is useful or relevant. Jesus' message of the coming of the Kingdom was effectively a "gospel" or "good News" (Mark 1:15) and "a power for salvation" (cf. Romans 1:16). Jesus doesn't just present us with a general truth, but he is the truth, and as such he is also the way to true life (John 14:6).

Different biblical images of Jesus

One reason why people perceive the Bible as irrelevant is that we keep using the same terms to explain what God has done for us. The most common image is the idea of the justification of the sinner. It explains that Christ died on the cross to take away our sins, so that we can be saved, and be righteous before God. This picture is taken directly from the Bible. If you understand that God is our Judge, and have recognized that compared with his holiness we are all guilty, this concept is profoundly liberating. That's why this message spoke so strongly to Jews in the time of Paul and to Christians in the time of Luther – one of the primary ways to understand God's relationship to us was in terms of God's justice and judgment.

However, this also shows us why this presentation doesn't appeal to unchurched people today. They may have a dim awareness of God, but even when they accept his existence they mostly major on the idea that God is love, that he encourages us and wants the best for us. The notion that we need Jesus before we can appear righteous before God doesn't connect with them at all. As a consequence, many Christians feel obliged to spend much of their evangelistic outreach explaining that we are sinners who cannot stand before God. The problem is that this is a negative message, with very little relevance to our listeners. They probably have no concept of an absolute moral order with which our lives should comply. They think justice is merely a human construct by which we regulate our society.

If we look more closely at the Bible we find that it uses many different images to talk about what Jesus has done for us.

Sin is compared to imprisonment and slavery, and Jesus is shown as the one who pays our ransom (Mark 10:45; 1 Peter 1:17–19). Or sin is compared to something that makes us ill, and Jesus is the doctor who heals us (Matthew 9:12). Evil reigns over our lives and Jesus is the one who liberates us from its power (Colossians 2:15). Many people who find it hard to picture God as a heavenly Judge can nevertheless relate to those images. They know what it is to be bound by destructive, addictive behaviour. In that light they can make sense of the Christ who liberates us from forces greater than ourselves. They find it easier to imagine that humanity is ill in some way, than that we are guilty before God. If we're following up this image, we can start by asking whether humanity's relationship with God might have something to do with our "illness".

Reconciliation is another significant biblical image which is much closer to contemporary experience. It implies a broken relationship and thus chimes with many people's painful lack of significant and stable relationships. When the Bible speaks of reconciliation, it presupposes that the most decisive relationship is the one between God and humanity: Jesus is the one who reconciles the two. Many people can't easily accept that relationship as the most important one of their lives. But they generally share the common understanding that no one can live without good relationships; this can form a stepping-stone to showing them that the Gospel isn't divorced from real life, but concerns us profoundly.

In fact, what God does for us in Jesus Christ is so multifaceted that the Bible needs many images to show its riches: Jesus is a rock for people who have no secure place to stand, and a shepherd for those who lack direction; he gives rest to those who are tired, comfort to those who mourn, and freedom to those who are enslaved. We could add many others. When we share the

Gospel, it's important to start with the images that resonate most deeply with the lives of our hearers. From there we can go on to other ideas which may be further removed from contemporary experience, yet can help deepen their understanding.

When we're looking for ways to explain who Jesus is, there's always a danger that we'll fall back on the formulations of the Gospel that were most important in our own faith development. If we want to share the relevance of the Gospel in fresh ways, we'll need to read the Bible with an open heart to discover the many aspects of what God has done for us. We will also need to make a real effort to read people at a deeper level, in order to understand their needs and build bridges between them and the Gospel.

Life in its fullness

The biblical message isn't relevant only because it offers answers to human needs. Many people don't feel their lives are particularly problematic. If we have to tell them that they've got more problems than they think, before we can start to proclaim the Gospel, then our message is going to sound very negative. Of course it's true that people have no idea how lost they are without God, but they won't easily accept that. Most people will simply reject the message, and subsequently they'll have no interest in continuing the conversation with you or any other Christian. Even if they realize that not everything in their lives runs smoothly, they'll still find it easier to ignore the problem.

The Bible shows us plenty of ways to share the message in a more positive way. The Gospel offers us a magnificent gift, the best a human being can ever receive. It enriches our lives in ways we would never think possible beforehand. It's a treasure worth everything we have (Matthew 13:44). It's eternal life – and in the Bible this means not just the continuation of life after death, but life in abundance, life in its fullness (John 10:10). That life begins when we get to know Jesus (John 17:3).

Compare the following two statements and ask yourself which one provides a more effective invitation for further conversation.

C. (1): *You may think your life has been quite successful, but do you realize that you could lose it all in a moment? And I suspect you've known much more emptiness and disappointment in your life than you're willing to admit to.*

C. (2): *Have you ever had the experience of discovering something completely unexpected, something you didn't even look for? For instance, when my first baby was born, I think I knew it would be amazing, but I couldn't have imagined the feeling of holding my boy for the first time. That's what it's like when you come to know God. People feel as if they've been given an incredible gift, one they had only the vaguest idea of beforehand.*

What difference do you make to God?

Concentrating on the question "Why bother?" is to a certain degree a concession to our times. Postmodern society isn't concerned about truth any more, but about relevance; not about what's good, but about what works well. This question is much less central in the Bible, where God is simply entitled to our obedience and service. It's important to realize this, because a faith which is based only on our own need of God risks losing its value and becoming nominal during the periods when life is treating us well. Young Christians often tell me: "When I'm lonely or when life's tough, it's really helpful to pray and I feel my faith makes a difference. But when everything's going well it's so easy to forget about God."

This is why churches do better when they stress that Jesus isn't only our Saviour, but also our Lord. Christians from those backgrounds show more enthusiasm for God, because he's not there just to pull them out of the abyss of their sin and hopelessness. In good times they can offer up to him all the good things they have. The biblical message is not only: "You need God", but also: "God is entitled to your love and service and he wants to use you to accomplish his plans!" We all need to hear that our existence isn't meaningless, to know we're needed and that our lives can make a difference.

Three possible responses to "Why bother?"

1. The Gospel is the answer to your deepest needs.
2. The Gospel opens the way to life in all its fullness.
3. It's equally legitimate to ask: "What difference do you make to God?"

Openings

It's not easy to talk about indifference, because indifferent people tend to be indifferent about their indifference! It's sometimes wiser to be patient and wait for another occasion when someone may be more open to talk about faith. People can be so absorbed by the rat race that they forget what's really important. Then they encounter something such as a midlife crisis, and realize there are moments when they want to ask: "Does any of this make sense?" "Why do I live like this?" "What forces me to live this way?" Yet we should, of course, always be looking for opportunities ourselves, however small, and use such moments as wisely and effectively as possible.

Your own life

It's because indifference makes meaningful conversations so hard to start that it's important that our own lives constitute an invitation to dialogue. Can people see that Jesus makes a radical difference to us? Can they see that our lives are richer, deeper, more exciting and more beautiful because we know him? It's not always self-evident. When you ask Christians what difference Jesus makes to them, they may answer that because of him they're God's children and will live eternally with him. That is of course central to the Gospel message, but many people today aren't sensitive to those issues. Does our reconciliation with God have clear and visible effects on the way we experience life, how we live with those around us and our family, how we respond to joys and disappointments, and to the pain of the larger world?

And when people see a difference, is it a positive one? Is our life in these areas challenging and inviting, or is it constrained and boring? Many non-Christians still believe that being a Christian mostly means that the good things in life are prohibited. Is it obvious that we've only abandoned certain things as a consequence of the better life we've discovered?

The Gospel provides a great deal that's highly relevant to people today, if only they could see it. It enables us to be affected by the needs of the world without losing hope. It frees us from the fruitlessness and emptiness of life without God. It helps us accept the pain that others cause us, while giving us strength to forgive and continue. It gives us the assurance that someone holds us even when everything around us collapses. These examples show that your life doesn't need to be a success story in order to be "a letter from Christ". There are plenty of success stories which people automatically distrust or consider unattainable for themselves. Much more appealing are the life stories that show how life can be fruitful, have depth, and be worthwhile without denying and running away from the pain in our lives and in the world.

Our lives are a useful example not only so people can see how important Jesus is to us. It's equally important that we stand alongside them and can empathize with their lack of interest in questions of faith. That's possible only if we realize that our enthusiasm and engagement with the Gospel may be far from obvious. Can you understand why people can't be bothered with belief in God in today's world, when they feel their lives are already full enough without him? If so, that can be a good way into further conversation, because we can identify with their indifference.

N.: You seem to live in a different world from me. All this talk about God and heaven simply doesn't make sense to me.

C.: I can understand you saying that. It's not as if I feel God close by all the time. It's often easier for me to forget about God than to believe in him. Everything around us conspires to make us forget God.

N.: Really? I thought faith came easily to you. So why do you believe?

C.: It's hard to answer that in a nutshell. One thing is that life seems so drab and dull when I forget about him. That's why I make a conscious effort to make space for him in my life.

When you have opportunities to talk about the difference it makes to believe in God, it can be hard to come up with a neat answer. As always, it's important to indicate from the outset that we can't answer everything at once. That way, we stop people thinking they've understood everything, and concluding that the Christian faith has nothing to offer them.

The life of the non-Christian

We can also look for ways to engage in meaningful conversation starting with our conversation partner's own life experience. The French philosopher Blaise Pascal said that every person has a God-shaped hole. Human beings are created to know God and will never find fulfilment and rest until they are in relationship with him. Saint Augustine said something similar: "You made us for yourself and our heart is restless until it finds rest in you." That doesn't mean everyone is actively looking for God. Many people try to fill this emptiness in their lives in other ways. But it remains true that all those other things can never give us true life or complete our quest for fulfilment. That can only be found in relationship with God, who made us so we might know and love him.

It can't be emphasized enough that we mustn't tell people bluntly that they don't know true fulfilment in their lives. Even if they recognized it themselves, they probably wouldn't appreciate it if we told them so. It's more respectful and more effective if we can help people in an unthreatening way to look critically at themselves. We can do that by getting alongside them, by being vulnerable, and by sharing our own and others' life stories. If we manage to do this, there are many experiences that can fan a desire for God. Let's consider some of them.

Most people can remember situations where they wanted something very much and thought that achieving it would bring them all they could wish for: an engagement, a new home, a promotion at work. Yet shortly after this wish was finally fulfilled, they found they had a new desire, and started working towards the next goal. They go on and on like this, not realizing that we all try to fill our lives with things that may be good in themselves, but can never give complete satisfaction. This can offer an opportunity to ask whether it's good to keep setting new goals, or whether we shouldn't take a while to ask ourselves what makes life worth living and brings true satisfaction and happiness. Does God have a role to play here?

It's noticeable that disappointments result not only from our failures, but also from our successes. We've already referred to the midlife crisis – an experience that's significant for people going through it, and also for those around them. You can ask young people how so many people endure the rat race for decades to fulfil their dreams, only to be disillusioned once they reach their goal. They might like to ponder whether it's possible to avoid working themselves to death for twenty-five years before wondering whether it was all worth it.

C.: I think we fool ourselves, and other people go along with it. We think, if only I'd got this or done that, I'd be happy. It's worth looking at people who've really "made it". Some of them despair when they're right at the peak of their success. They ask themselves whether this is all there is, and whether life's worth living. Maybe we can learn from that. Ordinary people like you and me can cover up our dissatisfaction, and promise ourselves things will be better in the future, but they can't do that any longer. Have you noticed that?

The question: "What's the point?" obviously gives us an opening, and not only with people suffering a midlife crisis. Look at this quote from Alice (age thirty-four):

At the moment I'm leading a life pretty much like what I dreamed of as a little girl. A loving husband, two adorable children, a beautiful house, no worries about money, good

friends. But whenever I think of life going on like this for
another thirty or forty years, I just want to scream.[3]

Many people have discovered that the important things in life
can easily be crowded out by the pressure of all the trivia. That
doesn't necessarily mean God is important to them, but there
are indications that he might be. Firstly, people often discover at
some point that relationships are more important to them than
material things. They sometimes learn this the hard way: how
many discover only after a divorce, or once their children have
grown up, that they neglected their family relationships because
their jobs absorbed them entirely? This comes into focus when
you start asking how you can find happiness: one of the keys
is knowing that other people know you and love you. How
marvellous, then, to know that the Creator of the universe loves
you and wants a relationship with you! Once you start exploring
this more deeply, you may even come to the conclusion that the
only reason to believe in the value of personal relationships is that
there is a personal God who has willed our existence. It may also
become clear that a relationship with this God who will never
let us down, not even at our death, helps us to build balanced
relationships with people around us, who might after all leave us
or die. Such matters obviously demand deeper conversations.

Another common reference point is the suffering in the
world. If we're honest, we recognize that we take pleasure in
the small joys of our lives only by shutting ourselves off from
the rest of the world. Some of us lead sheltered lives, where we
simply forget about all the suffering and despair in the wider
world, and even about the people near to us who are in pain
because of the failure of their marriage, their work, their health,
or whatever. It's largely a consequence of the affluent lives we
lead in the West that so many of us can shut out the pain of

others and avoid thinking about God. But we need to question whether this is fair to all those other people, and whether this attitude is wise, considering the precariousness of our own lives. If we're honest, we might conclude that we suppress our questions about the fragility of our own well-being and our awareness of the suffering of others, because of a deep-seated fear that there may be no answers. Wouldn't it be better to consider seriously whether Jesus is the answer after all?

This chapter about indifference reveals again what has been our guiding principle all along in considering the many objections people raise against the Christian faith. Apologetic witness can't be effective and doesn't do justice to people when we concentrate on finding knock-down arguments and answers. We have to ask what motivates people to ask these questions or what has made them into people who can't even be bothered to ask them.

Trying to find such arguments doesn't do justice to the Gospel either. The Gospel isn't just a general truth about what the world is like; it is about God searching out the particular people we encounter right where they are in their unique personal history. Yet if we take people seriously, there should be a place for looking for the right answers and arguments too. We have reasons for the hope we have. Our faith in Christ is not just a beautiful story that appeals to optimistic people. It's God's liberating truth for all of us.

Questions for groups and for personal reflection

1. Can you empathize with religious indifference or do you find it incomprehensible? What do you think are the main causes of indifference to God?

2. Jesus forgives our sins, redeems us from slavery and imprisonment, heals us from all that ruins our lives, reconciles us with God, and is the way to life in all its fullness. Which of those images speaks most strongly to you and why? Think about some of the people with whom you've shared the Gospel. Would one of these images help them to understand better what Jesus does for us? Why that one in particular?

3. According to the Gospel of John, eternal life is not just something that comes after death, but something that starts the moment we come to Christ. It's life in all its fullness, life as rich as we can imagine. Try to express in words that a non-Christian could understand why life with Jesus is so much richer than life without him.

4. According to Pascal, everyone has a God-shaped hole – an empty space in their heart which only God can fill. Can you give examples of experiences that point to this emptiness, even if people try to cover it up? How can you explain this to other people in a non-threatening way?

5. Imagine you've been asked to read a passage from the Bible and share some thoughts about it at a welcome dinner for non-Christians. You choose the parable of the hidden treasure (Matthew 13:44). How could you explain that the message of the Kingdom of God is so special that you would give up everything else for it?

Notes

1. (p. 49) This example is from Nicky Gumbel, *Searching Issues: Tackling Seven Common Objections to the Christian Faith*, Eastbourne: Kingsway, 1994, p. 21.

2. (p. 157) This quote is from Govert Buijs, "Waar doe je het allemaal voor? Zinvragen in gesprekken met andersgelovigen" in T. C. Verhoef (ed.), *Over de brug komen: Een handreiking voor het getuigend gesprek*, Zoetermeer: Boekencentrum, 1996, pp. 43–44.

3. (p.167) This quote is from Govert Buijs, "Waar doe je het allemaal voor? Zinvragen in gesprekken met andersgelovigen" in T. C. Verhoef (ed.), *Over de brug komen: Een handreiking voor het getuigend gesprek*, Zoetermeer: Boekencentrum, 1996, p. 44.

For Further Reading

Chapter 1: "Why Do You Believe?"

David K. Clark, *Dialogical Apologetics: A Person-Centered Approach to Christian Defense*, Grand Rapids: Baker, 1993.

Michael Green, *Evangelism through the Local Church*, London: Hodder & Stoughton, 1990.

Nicky Gumbel, *Searching Issues: Tackling Seven Common Objections to the Christian Faith*, Eastbourne: Kingsway, 1994.

Alister E. McGrath, *Bridge-Building: Effective Christian Apologetics*, Leicester: IVP, 1992.

Peter Kreeft & Ronald K. Tacelli, *Handbook of Christian Apologetics: Hundreds of Answers to Crucial Questions*, Crowborough: Monarch, 1995.

John G. Stackhouse, *Humble Apologetics: Defending the Faith Today*, Oxford, New York et al.: Oxford University Press, 2002.

Chapter 2: "Can't You Understand?"

Os Guinness, *Doubt*, 3rd edition, Tring: Lion Publishing, 1987.

Alister E. McGrath, *Doubt: Handling it Honestly*, Leicester: IVP, 1990.

Alister E. McGrath, *Bridge-Building: Effective Christian Apologetics*, Leicester: IVP, 1992, pp. 95–131.

Alister E. McGrath & Michael Green, *Springboard for Faith*, London: Hodder & Stoughton, 1993.

Nick Pollard, *Evangelism Made Slightly Less Difficult: How to Interest People Who Aren't Interested*, Leicester: IVP, 1997.

Wim Rietkerk, *If Only I Could Believe!*, Carlisle: Paternoster, 1997.

Chapter 3: "What About Suffering?"

The distinction between the different biblical responses to suffering is gleaned from: Nicky Gumbel, *Searching Issues: Tackling Seven Common Objections to the Christian Faith*, Eastbourne: Kingsway, 1994.

See also: C. S. Lewis, *The Problem of Pain*, London: Geoffrey Bless, 1947.

C. S. Lewis, *A Grief Observed*, London: Faber and Faber, 1966. Lewis wrote his second book on suffering after the death of his wife, when the more intellectual answers of his first book were no longer sufficient. It is sometimes said that this indicates that for Lewis the first book was now obsolete. However, Lewis never rejected his first book and in my opinion we should understand the second book as a different answer for a different situation.

Philip Yancey, *Where Is God When it Hurts?*, Grand Rapids: Zondervan, 2001.

Chapter 4: "Everyone's Entitled to Their Opinion"

Donald A. Carson, *The Gagging of God: Christianity Confronts Pluralism*, Leicester: IVP, 1996.

Lesslie Newbigin, *The Gospel in a Pluralist Society*, London: SPCK, 1989.

Chapter 5: "Aren't All Religions the Same?"

Norman Anderson, *Christianity and the World Religions: The Challenge of Pluralism*, Leicester: IVP, 1984.

Vinoth Ramachandra, *Faiths in Conflict?*, Leicester: IVP, 1999.

Chris Wright, *What's So Unique about Jesus?*, Eastbourne: MARC, 1990.

Chapter 6: "Just Prove It!"

Del Ratzsch, *Science and Its Limits: The Natural Sciences in Christian Perspective*, Leicester: Apollos (IVP), 2000.

Michael J. Murray (ed.), *Reason for the Hope Within*, Grand Rapids: Eerdmans, 1999.

John Polkinghorne, *One World: The Interaction of Science and Theology*, London: SPCK, 1986.

Anthony Flew, *There is a God: How the World's Most Notorious Atheist Changed His Mind*, New York: HarperOne, 2007.

Chapter 7: "Why Jesus?"

David Burke, *Jesus Unplugged*, Leicester: IVP, 2000.

Michael Green, *The Empty Cross of Jesus*, new edition, London: Hodder & Stoughton, 1998.

Alister E. McGrath, *Knowing Christ*, London: Hodder & Stoughton, 2001.

Philip Yancey, *The Jesus I Never Knew*, new edition, Grand Rapids: Zondervan, 2000.

Chapter 8: "Why Bother?"

Alister E. McGrath, *Bridge-Building: Effective Christian Apologetics*, Leicester: IVP, 1992, pp. 17–30, 51–75.

Alister E. McGrath, *Making Sense of the Cross*, Leicester: IVP, 1992.

Thomas V. Morris, *Making Sense of it All: Pascal and the Meaning of Life*, Grand Rapids: Eerdmans, 1992, pp. 15–45, 129–44.